STEEL CITY PRESS

This first edition published in 2019 by Steel City Press.

ISBN 978-1-913047-00-9

Proudly printed in the United Kingdom.

INDEX

INTRODUCTION

I'm finishing writing this book in January 2019, and it'll be published in mid-January 2019, so hopefully it'll be pretty up-to-date when it comes out.

Whether you voted Remain or Leave in the referendum, or even if you didn't vote at all, the next two months are going to be critical to the future of our country.

The aim of this book is to help you to understand more about what's going on with Brexit. I've believed in, and campaigned for, Brexit since before the word Brexit was invented. However, I'm going to write a little more neutrally in this book. If you're looking for a superficial book that mirrors everything that you already believe, you've come to the wrong place.

What I'm trying to do is give you an understanding of what's going on behind the scenes with Brexit - to explain *why* people are acting the way they are, even when I might totally disagree with what they're doing or saying.

Do you think most politicians have done an appalling job in negotiating Brexit? So do I, but I'm going to try to explain the thinking behind it. If you understand what's going on, it'll give you insight and an edge with your thinking.

I've met many of the people involved in negotiations - both big names, and behind the scenes. As a Member of the European

Parliament, I've heard exactly what EU politicians are saying behind closed doors as well as in public. I've made my fair share of scathing speeches, telling them exactly what I think when I believe they're wrong. I've been interviewed by many of the top journalists in print and on TV. I've done the detailed stuff too - I've read and submitted amendments to European Parliament resolutions on Brexit. I've read Theresa May's draft 585-page Withdrawal Agreement and the judgements in the various court cases, and I've given evidence on Brexit to a House of Lords Select Committee.

I've tried not to make the book too complicated (well, apart from the chapters that *have* to be a bit more technical, such as the ones on the court cases and Northern Ireland). Please don't shoot the messenger either: when I'm explaining how politicians are thinking, don't think I'm intending to excuse their actions. I'm certainly not! But I've left you, the reader, to draw your own inferences from the information available. After all, you are the jury. You're the people who will have to decide at future elections whether you've got the right politicians - or the wrong ones.

Where Brexiteers have made mistakes too (and they have), I've pointed those out too. You might not even enjoy reading this book. When I've shown extracts to friends and family, it's often made them angry at how politicians could let the public down so badly.

What I can promise, I hope, is that you'll learn something from reading this book. If this book helps people to understand the maze of nonsense we've seen in the last couple of years, it will have been well worth the effort of writing it.

CHAPTER 1

WHAT IS BREXIT?
(AND WHY THAT'S NOT ACTUALLY AS STUPID A QUESTION AS IT SOUNDS)

We've all heard the word Brexit. It's one of those words that many people are growing quite sick of hearing. At first sight, it's not exactly difficult to know what it's supposed to mean. **Br**itish **Exit** from the European Union. That much is pretty clear. The problem comes in defining what that actually means.

If I were to choose a random sample of a hundred people and start asking them questions like these, I would suddenly start to hear real disagreement over what it means. In some cases, people might not fully understand the questions. Is it still Brexit if...

- *If EU courts still have the power to overrule UK courts?*
- *If the UK does not regain the power to strike its own independent trade deals?*
- *If the UK still has to obey EU laws?*
- *If the UK still participates in European Union programmes?*
- *If the UK is still in the European Economic Area (EEA) or the European Free Trade Area (EFTA)?*
- *If the UK is still in the Single Market or the Customs Union?*
- *If the UK is still part of the European Court of Human Rights?*

What's even harder is that when you look at Theresa May's deal, nobody could actually give you a straight yes or no answer to whether those situations will actually happen. I've read all 585 pages of the Withdrawal Agreement. I've read the whole Political Declaration, and the Attorney General's advice. Even working out whether some of those things are happpening or not isn't straightforward.

Will EU courts be able to overrule UK courts? The short answer is that, like a Facebook relationship status, 'it's complicated'. The UK will be required to obey some EU laws, at the very least, during the so-called Transition Period (but more of that later). Afterwards, it's an even more grey area: there's plenty of times where the Withdrawal Agreement requires the UK to have laws with similar effect to the EU's laws. What does that mean, exactly? Who rules on what EU laws mean? That one's simple enough to answer: the EU courts do.

So EU courts won't directly be able to overrule UK courts, but UK courts will have to follow decisions of the EU's courts.

Everything's complicated when it comes to this Withdrawal Agreement. It's designed to be complicated. It's designed not to be easy for someone to just sit down, read, and understand. The first time I read it, I couldn't possibly understand it. The Agreement doesn't specify what things mean, unless you've read the relevant EU legislation. Take this as an example - from Article 41(2) of the Withdrawal Agreement:

The requirements set out in Articles 34 and 35 TFEU and the relevant Union law governing the marketing of goods, including the conditions for the marketing of goods, applicable to the goods concerned shall apply in respect of the goods referred to in paragraph 1.

What does that mean? Well, as it happens it means that neither side could put 'quantitative restrictions' on imports or exports of goods that are in transit at the end of the Transition Period. But you don't know that until you've read the whole Article, looked up the relevant legislation for yourself, and checked what it actually means. So it's not just a case of reading a 585-page document. It's a case of reading that document *and every single piece of EU legislation referred to in that document.*

But if I read the 585 pages, and if I read all the legislation that it refers to, I'll understand what's going on, right...?

Actually, you probably wouldn't understand it even then. Because what each piece of legislation actually means in practice depends on how you interpret it. And it's the European Court of Justice that does the interpreting.

Now take that and notice that some things are expected to still apply, pretty much forever, even after the end of the Transition Period.

Like I said, it's complicated. And that's just the question about the EU courts.

The same 'well, sort of' answer comes when you ask whether the

UK will be able to strike up its own independent trade deals with third countries under the Withdrawal Agreement. The answer is legally 'yes', but in practice 'no'. The future relationship with the European Union wouldn't let us provide favourable terms for goods, but it would let us do a trade deal based on services.

The trouble is, that we tend to buy goods from the rest of the world and sell them services. The trade deals we want to do basically look like this: 'We'll agree to let businesses buy your stuff easily, if you agree to let your businesses buy services from us'.

The UK is the second-biggest exporter of services in the world. No country in its right mind is going to want to do a services-only deal with us. They want to be able to sell us goods, and in exchange they'll let us sell them services.

Don't get me wrong, we can already buy and sell stuff without having to negotiate trade deals. It's just that there are then taxes (tariffs) placed on imports, which makes things that we import more expensive to buy.

What does all this mean? Well, it means that when Theresa May says something like 'the UK will regain the legal power to sign trade deals with other countries', she's telling the truth - but it's purely theoretical. When her opponents say 'we won't actually be able to negotiate any good trade deals in practice', they're telling the truth too.

By this point, you're probably thinking that this whole thing is way too complex. You'd be right. It's a fudge that took years to make. If Theresa May gets her way, then...

We'll have the power to negotiate trade deals - but we won't really.

We'll stop the EU courts' ability to overrule UK courts, but UK courts will still have to rule according to EU law.

We'll still be participating in EU programmes, but not actually being members of them.

I know a lot of people who'd say 'The Withdrawal Agreement isn't actually Brexit', and I know others who'd say that it definitely is Brexit.

One of the odd quirks of all this is that (generally) Remain supporters are more likely to say that it is Brexit, whilst on the other hand Leave supporters are more likely to say that it is not. That, of course, is part of the battle that's being fought at the moment. Both sides want to define what Brexit actually is.

CHAPTER 2

WHY IS BRITAIN DIFFERENT IN THE FIRST PLACE?

There's certainly anti-EU feeling across the continent of Europe. In Italy and Greece, there's bad feeling about the European Union's actions in relation to their debts. In Catalonia, the EU's actions relating to their independence from Spain keeps the EU relatively unpopular. There's bad feeling, as seen recently with the so-called 'Gilets Jaunes' protests, in France - feeling which is aimed primarily at domestic politicians, but also at the EU. In some Eastern European countries, there's further bad feeling about migration. Anti-EU or eurosceptic parties are on the rise in other countries, have made breakthroughs in Denmark, Holland, Sweden, Austria and many others, and are set to make big gains in the 2019 elections. Even in the staunchly pro-EU Republic of Ireland, a new anti-EU party has been set up. Euroscepticism is generally the preserve of the Right and the Left but not of the Centre; that's because in Europe coalition government is the norm. If the Centre is used to being in power in one form or another, then it's probably okay with an EU system which basically supports their own consensus. Therefore, euroscepticism rises on the Right and Left; centrist voices find it difficult to get a eurosceptic party going.

Yes, euroscepticism in one form or another is on the rise. But there's something different in Britain. You wouldn't, at the moment, expect any other nation to actually vote to leave the European Union. There might be nations which regret joining the euro, nations which regret being a part of the Schengen Area, and much more. They haven't - at least yet - got to a situation where a majority of the people would be likely to vote to leave the European Union.

So why is Britain different? Is it just an example of exceptionalism to suggest that we are somehow different to the EU27, or is there actually a genuine reason to believe that there's something different which is driving this extra step?

Actually, I think there are a few powerful explanations for this difference:

1. Our trade is different

The UK does more of our trade with non-EU countries than we do with EU countries. This isn't true of the vast majority of the EU27. They generally do their trade within Europe. The UK is different because of geography (we don't share a land border with continental Europe, unless you count the Channel Tunnel), because of our historic links with the Commonwealth, because of our historic links with the USA, and because of the nature of our economy.

Generally speaking, being in the Customs Union and Single Market makes day-to-day trade with EU countries easier. We'd have to follow EU legislation if we wanted to sell things to the EU anyway - we just wouldn't have to follow it for the vast majority of the time when we're not selling things to the EU. Most of the trade we do is either internal (UK businesses trading with other UK businesses) or with third countries (UK businesses trading with non-EU

11

businesses). If you're a country that is doing 70% of its international trade with other EU countries, the small extra convenience for the 70% might outweigh the 30% which isn't quite so convenient. You might even stretch a point and try to claim that the internal trade is okay following those rules because of supply chains and so on.

If you're the UK, doing only 45% or so of our international trade with the EU (and in practice, it's actually less, because of a neat piece of statistical chicanery that I'll tell you about in a moment), then the negative impact on the 55% might well outweigh any positive impact on the 45% - and it certainly does, when you think about businesses that don't trade internationally at all.

2. Our economy is different

The UK is a huge net importer when it comes to goods, but we're net exporters of services. Our economy relies upon the City of London. So when (for example) the European Union wants to introduce the Financial Transaction Tax, and the Common Consolidated Corporate Tax Base, that's something which would drive business away from the UK and to the USA. It might hurt other EU members a little bit, but it would hurt the United Kingdom far, far more.

3. The island mentality (but not in the way that you think)

This isn't a 'little Englander' type argument. It's actually more a point about the nature of other nations. Take the city of Strasbourg for example. It's been French, it's been German, and it's been French again. When national borders have fluctuated over the years, when a city might have been in one country and then another, there's less of a sense that the national identity should be something to be particularly cherished. Borders which haven't persisted for long don't lend themselves to being borders. Someone who lives in France, but considers themselves just as German as they do French, might well be particularly keen that there's no hard border between France and Germany.

This sort of fluidity of borders and nationality, the allegiance to regions being almost as powerful as allegiance to nations, doesn't really lend itself to a feeling that the nation state isn't being protected. The thought of transferring power from nation state to the European Union feels different somehow.

4. The British people had different expectations of the EU

In other European countries, principles like 'ever-closer union' haven't been kept particularly secret from the general public. The notion that once power has been given to the European Union, it will never be returned to the nation state, is a principle which feels more normal to people from other European countries than it does to people from the UK.

Part of the reason for this can be traced all the way back to the 1970s, when the UK joined the EU (or, and this distinction actually matters, what was then called the Common Market). The 1972 European Communities Act took us into the European Union (that Act will crop back up again later), and we entered the Common Market in 1973. Having cut other trading links and ties, including with the Commonwealth, the government then decided to offer the British people a referendum in 1975 about whether to stay in the Common Market or not. The British people at the time believed that they were voting for a trading organisation, not for (in effect) what has become European government, with the EU having the ability to pass laws across almost every area of daily life.

That disconnect between what people thought they were voting for, and what they actually got, sowed the seeds of the anti-European Union movement in the UK. This is the reasoning behind (for example) the anti-Federalist League - the precursor to UKIP - being set up. Because the 'product' people voted for was so different from the 'product' that they received, the 'brand' of the European Union was tarnished in the UK right from the beginning. The British people had always had something of an ambivalent view of the Common Market. For example, you can find plenty of Winston Churchill quotes which support the principle of greater European unity, but you can equally find Churchill quotes which say that the UK should always choose (for example) the deep blue sea over Europe.

Churchill may have believed in the necessity of something like the EU for continental Europe, but there's a difference between believing in post-war co-operation between those European nations, and wanting the UK to be a member of the kind of organisation which the EU has now become.

Right from the start, I think it's fair to say that the European Union was built upon a foundation of sand where popular opinion in the UK was concerned. No attempts were really made to change this until a number of decades later.

5. *The Exchange Rate Mechanism*

Going back to the 1975 referendum on the Common Market, the government at the time led by Harold Wilson sent a leaflet to every house in the country saying this:

"There was a threat to employment in Britain from the movement in the Common Market towards an Economic & Monetary Union. This could have forced us to accept fixed exchange rates for the pound, restricting industrial growth and putting jobs at risk. This threat has been removed."

So when, in the early 1990s, the UK joined what was then known as the Exchange Rate Mechanism ('the euro without the notes and coins'), suddenly there was surprise within the UK. Economic and Monetary Union was something that the British people had been told would not happen, but the UK now had precisely that: fixed exchange rates between the pound and other European countries.

Pro-euro campaigners claimed later (and with some justification) that the UK fixed the exchange rate at the wrong level. This, in a nutshell, might be argued by Greece when they're in the euro. The consequences of the Exchange Rate Mechanism were brutal. The UK economy was devastated as 100,000 businesses went bankrupt and unemployment doubled. The UK crashed out of the Exchange Rate Mechanism, and the levels of trust were damaged beyond repair. The whole situation led to a severe backlash against the Conservative

Party, which had just won the 1992 election unexpectedly. The stage was set for a Labour landslide in 1997, which brought Tony Blair to power. By this time, the British people felt that they'd had a lucky escape from what was going to become the euro.

Unfortunately, the Labour Party at the time were rather keen on joining the euro - and the Conservative Party, which you'd expect perhaps to be rather reticent after the Exchange Rate Mechanism debacle, was not absolutely opposed to it.

A new political party set up, to demand that any government must commit to a referendum before attempting to join the euro. Both Labour and the Conservatives pledged one; the Referendum Party, having achieved its main objective, didn't make its hoped-for splash. It had, however, changed the future of British politics.

With the UK not joining the euro, there was further divergence between the UK and the rest of the European Union. It had also paved the way for Prime Minister Tony Blair.

6. EU enlargement and the English language

Immigration, before Tony Blair, had been running at around 20,000-30,000 net annually. By the end of the Labour government, net immigration was around ten times as high - and there it has stayed ever since.

In 2004, the European Union added ten new countries. European Union rules require so-called 'free movement of workers', which is one of the 'four freedoms of the European Union'. This means that between any nations within the European Union, four things - people, goods, services and capital - must be able to move freely. A citizen of one Member State could move to live and work in any other Member State, with few restrictions.

One of the key restrictions was this: for the first 5 years, any country could retain restrictions on immigration from new countries joining the European Union. The new nations were mainly poorer countries; even well-educated workers could seek to improve their lot by coming to work in the UK on minimum wage.

The Tony Blair government was one of only three European governments which didn't exercise its right to those restrictions. The Blair government miscalculated, assuming that only 5,000 to 13,000 people would come to the UK. The true figure was in the hundreds of thousands.

As with the Common Market and the Exchange Rate Mechanism before, this further eroded trust and confidence in the European Union.

The idea of 'free movement of workers' is fairly straightforward in one sense: it assumes that migration flows will work two ways, and be roughly balanced. But there's a problem with that: the English language. Whether you're from France or Poland, Greece or Spain, Romania or Portugal, when you learn a foreign language in school, that language is almost certain to be English. English being a global language, it's almost universally taught and learned.

Now, put yourself in the shoes of someone from one of the poorest EU countries looking to move to a richer country to make money and send that money home to family. Would you go to Germany, or Slovenia, Sweden, France, or Belgium, where you don't speak the local language? Of course you would not. You'd go to the UK - because you can already speak some English.

But if you were a British citizen looking to move abroad, there's no obvious choice that stands out.

For this reason, by the time of the referendum there were around 3.2 million EU nationals living in the UK - compared with around 1.2 million British citizens living in other EU countries. An imbalance had been created, and that imbalance impacted upon the jobs market - and on wages. Everything the government had promised in the referendum campaign of 1975 now seemed so far from reality.

7. The legal systems don't match

This is the most technical reason, but it's actually quite important - more important than most people would give it credit for. The UK legal system is very different to that of continental Europe. It's based upon Magna Carta rather than the Napoleonic code.

Now, imagine that you're the European Union writing Directives and Regulations. It doesn't always cause any problem to the UK (in this sense) when the EU uses Directives. Directives tell countries what they must do (your laws must ensure that X, Y and Z happens). They're based more upon outcomes than upon how to achieve them.

On the other hand, Regulations become law directly in the Member States. They then end up being interpreted by the courts in the Member States. The European Union prefers Regulations because of this: they're European laws rather than relying on domestic laws to interpret them. But Regulations cause more problems in the UK because our legal system is different.

Either way, problems could arise with regard to the differences in legal systems. Directive 80/181/EC was updated and amended on a number of occasions, but it eventually required the UK (from 2000) to ban the sale of goods in imperial measurements alone.

When some market traders declined to obey the EU law, they were prosecuted under criminal law. That was the nature of how the UK's legal system interpreted the Directive. Had it been pretty much any other nation (which wouldn't have wanted to use imperial measures anyway), penalties would have been civil rather than criminal.

These little differences led to something called 'gold-plating', where new EU laws would become even more onerous by the time they'd been written into UK law. It made the European Union more unpopular in the UK than it had been.

There are other arguments which could be made in respect of explaining the reasons for the Brexit vote. I haven't yet mentioned fishing or farming, for example. I suppose that fishing would count as being something different about the UK - simply because the UK has such a high percentage of the value of all the fish in Europe. Therefore, our resource finds itself being shared between the

European Union - whilst our fish stocks suffer, and our fishermen are put out of business. But in general, in this chapter I've tried to only mention the reasons why popular opinion in the UK is substantially out of kilter with popular opinion in other European Union countries.

The fact that the UK's approach differs from the EU's is clear: the UK has been outvoted more than any other country in the Council of Ministers, for example. The UK stayed out of the Schengen Area and the euro. If anything, it's been self-evident for decades that the UK has different approaches to the European Union in a number of areas.

Sooner or later, something was going to have to happen to change that. Talk of a so-called 'two-speed Europe', where some nations would have a looser relationship with the EU whilst others would have a stronger one, never really got off the ground. Nobody ever resolved the many issues which existed within the European Union.

Remain supporters admitted that the European Union needed to be reformed; that much at least was common ground. Leave campaigners replied by saying that the UK had been trying to reform it for 40 years, and that things had got worse in that time rather than better.

CHAPTER 3

WAS IMMIGRATION THE REASON FOR BREXIT?

The answer to this question, like to many other questions about Brexit, is 'sort of'. There are so many contradictory findings from opinion polls over the last couple of years that it's difficult to separate the wood from the trees.

Whether immigration, or democracy/sovereignty, is given as the number one motivator for the Leave vote generally depends on how the question is asked. Part of the reason for this is that a vote for Brexit intending to regain sovereignty would normally also include a belief that the UK should (at least) have greater control over the system of immigration from the European Union. It's just that a vote based primarily on sovereignty might not place immigration quite so high on the list.

Take, for example, a Survation poll from October 2016 on the reasons why people voted for Leave and why people voted Remain. They found that 47.8% of Brexit voters put immigration as their number one reason for voting for Brexit, and that 74.7% of Brexit voters had it amongst their top three reasons. The second-placed option, that 'Leaving the European Union is the only way that the UK can make its own laws and control its destiny', was placed as the number one reason by 25.1% of Brexit voters, whilst 58.8% placed it somewhere within the top three reasons. At first sight, you'd say that this is evidence that immigration (whilst not the only reason) was clearly by far the dominant reason for the Brexit vote. But a further 6.2% placed 'the EU is a corrupt racket' as their number one reason (23.8% had it among their top three), 3.3% had a desire to free the UK from red tape (25.4% had it amongst their top three), and so on.

These options are all to do with regaining sovereignty, and there are a couple of others in that poll. What's actually surprising, given the furore since the referendum about the so-called 'Boris bus', is that just 6.7% gave 'Leaving would save the UK money which could be spent at home' as their number one reason for voting to Leave.

It's difficult to make any sense of the 'among the top three', because if you add together the figures, they'll (naturally) add up to more than 100% because people chose more than one option. The only obvious conclusions to be drawn from the whole poll are that a) immigration was a substantial driver of the Leave vote, and that b) Almost half of Brexit voters gave it as their number one reason for voting for Brexit.

Let's take a hypothetical scenario. Suppose that before the referendum, the European Union had offered the UK a concession on immigration - allowing the UK to suspend the 'free movement of people'. Perhaps in our alternate universe they offered a fudge, along the lines of allowing the UK to limit numbers (because of the asymmetry discussed in the previous chapter). In such a case, would the UK still have voted to Leave?

I suspect not: the referendum result was close, with a vote of around 51.8%-48.2% in favour of Brexit. If the immigration argument had been partly resolved, just enough to persuade a few percent of those Brexit voters for whom immigration was their main reason for voting Leave, then the referendum result would probably have been Remain.

I used to be a Mathematics teacher, some years ago. One important principle in Mathematics is something known as *necessary and sufficient conditions*.

So if you hear thunder, that is *sufficient* to know that there's been lightning; you don't get thunder without lightning.

On the other hand, it's not *necessary*. You can see lightning without having heard the thunder.

In Maths, we often looked for something being both necessary and sufficient at the same time. We'd say things like 'A is true, if and only if B is true'.

If it's Christmas Day, then it's December 25th. If it's December 25th, then it's Christmas Day. So it being December 25th is both necessary and sufficient for it to be Christmas Day.

In this sense, I might well say that the immigration issue was a *necessary* part of the conditions for a Leave vote at the referendum.

But was it also *sufficient*? Could Brexit have happened if immigration was the only reason for people voting to Leave? In that case, I think the answer is very clearly 'no'.

I said earlier that the polling is a bit contradictory in places. When a Lord Ashcroft poll immediately after the referendum asked Leave voters to rank their reasons for leaving, the answers were different.

This time, the rankings were pretty much the reverse of Survation's findings. 'The principle that decisions about the UK should be taken in the UK' was ranked first, by 49% of voters. That was, in essence, an issue of sovereignty/democracy. Meanwhile, 'A feeling that voting to leave the EU offered the best chance for the UK to regain control over immigration and its own borders' was ranked first by just 30% of respondents.

I should point out here that in both cases, we're talking about polls that are mathematically weighted to ensure that they're as representative as possible of the general public. It's not like an online 'poll' where people self-select and decide whether to take part, introducing bias. Proper opinion polls, even those by firms purporting to follow British Polling Council rules, can sometimes still be biased, but I don't think that bias is the explanation here.

I think that the complex relationship between the different reasons for voting to Leave is such that people answer the question slightly differently, depending on how it's asked.

Just before the referendum, the British Election Study asked a similar question but unprompted. Rather than giving people a list of statements to choose from, they instead asked people to give their own reasons. They then put those reasons into categories. This time, the top two reasons - immigration and sovereignty - were tied for 'first place' when it comes to explaining people's reasons for voting for Brexit.

I think I'm perfectly justified in saying that immigration as an issue was *necessary but not sufficient* to cause a vote for Brexit.

You might accuse me of not really answering the question at the start of this chapter though. Immigration may not have been the only reason for the referendum vote to leave, but there's a wider question: was immigration the reason we had the referendum in the first place?

Think about it this way: if it had not been for Tony Blair's (and, to a lesser extent, Gordon Brown's) approach towards immigration from 1997 to 2010, would the levels of anger towards the European Union that caused David Cameron to capitulate and offer a referendum have still been there?

Let's remember that at much of the relevant time, immigration was one of the top 2 or 3 issues in British politics. Every month, MORI would do what they called a 'political issues index' which tracked over time which issues are considered most important by the general public. Over the first 15 years of this century, immigration was pretty much consistently there in the top three - sometimes being the number one issue.

Others came and went; at different times, crime, the economy, the NHS, and defence/terrorism would be there. Immigration, though, was a constant. This is something that people haven't really fully become aware of. If we go back to the 1990s, prior to the Blair government, then immigration would consistently be very low down the list of priorities. Quite often, it wouldn't even feature in the top ten issues in voters' concerns. Even in 1997, in the four months before the General Election at which Tony Blair was elected Prime Minister, immigration was considered the most important issue by no more than 3% of people.

In August 1999, it hit 10% for the first time in many years - but that turned out to be just a blip, at least for the time being. By 2001, it would not fall under 10% for the entire year.

The figures for 2003/2004 onwards, around the time that the EU enlargement occurred and the UK opened its borders to the so-called A8 countries, saw immigration jump to being seen by (on average) 30% as the most important issue in British politics.

From there, immigration considered to be a huge issue. It dominated political discussions. Immigration had become synonymous with the European Union; that was never going to change.

It was against this backdrop that the BNP - a (frankly) racist party started to build its support. When so many people had concerns over immigration, it was saddening - but not surprising - that people turned to an extreme. For those 30% of people, none of the major political parties at that time were speaking their language. It only took a small percentage of those 30%, before the British National Party (BNP) started to rise substantially. They started to gain Council seats and even managed to take two seats at the European

Parliament elections in 2009. The political establishment didn't react well: if you react by hectoring voters and telling them that they're racist, you'll turn them against you. Rather than defeat the BNP in open debate, they chose instead to attack those who voted for them. The problem? They'd just created a subsection of the community who would forever hate them.

Worse still, those within the 30% who rejected the BNP felt that their concerns were being marginalised. Their views were being wrongly associated with the BNP. This didn't drive them into the arms of the BNP, but it left them feeling that they didn't really have a political party to vote for.

The immigration issue led to an anti-establishment feeling. Those two combined to deliver the conditions necessary for Brexit to happen.

Thankfully, the BNP was ultimately utterly defeated. It started to turn in on itself, with different factions and splinter parties breaking off on a regular basis.

The main reason for that was that - in the absence of a moderate, reasonable party articulating genuine concerns over uncontrolled mass net immigration - the BNP had attracted some people who voted for it out of pure desperation. That desperation manifested itself in some rather unusual ways. I recall, at one all-up Council election, seeing some ballot papers where people had used one vote to vote Green, and another to vote BNP. You'd think that the two would have little in common to appeal to voters, but the principle of anti-establishment voting had begun.

When UKIP (and UKIP was a very, very different organisation then than it is today) made its way back onto the political scene after the expenses scandal in 2009, it was prepared to speak about immigration - but in a more reasoned way, one which reached more of that 30% of the electorate. Their message was more than just the 'Say No to European Union' that it had been back in 2004. UKIP had entered a yo-yo politics phase: it gained seats in 1999 at the European elections, then fell back into obscurity for the 2001 General Elections. It degenerated into infighting, then came back and gained more seats in 2004 at the European elections. A weak showing in 2005 at the General Election accompanied further infighting. It had a resurgence at the 2009 European elections, then fell back in 2010. Some of that was, of course, to do with the difficulties faced by smaller parties under the First Past The Post system - and the advantages of proportional representation.

But then, in 2011, something changed. UKIP moved substantially beyond the EU/immigration debate, and started talking about other things. The points which had been pushed by a few people (myself included, but also Pete Reeve, Lisa Duffy, Paul Nuttall and others) over a number of years about the need to work at Council elections started to develop some traction. The party started speaking out on other issues: it said things about crime, about the economy, about the education system and so on.

Now, for the first time, it started to make inroads at other kinds of elections too. In 2012, it started to pick up a few Council seats - but more importantly, its national share of the vote where it stood was creeping up. From 98,000 votes in England in 2008, in 2012 it took 220,000. This was an average of 13.8% where it stood; for the first time, the vote share began to challenge the established parties (the Lib Dem national vote share being 16%).

At the time, few people noticed because it didn't take many seats under First Past The Post. The establishment parties didn't see the threat. By 2013, opinion polls and canvass returns were starting to alert other parties and the media that something major was going on. UKIP were in the midst of a logistical exercise on a scale they had never undertaken before, putting almost 1,800 candidates into the field on a single day. The vetting process required was far beyond the Party's size.

Front-page headlines alerted the Party to people who shouldn't have been selected, or to those who - after being selected - did or said something so inappropriate that they had to be deselected. The media had woken up. The Party took swift action against any such extremists.

In one case, the media 'exposed' a UKIP candidate purportedly making a Nazi salute. The claim would have been laughable were it not so serious. The newspaper concerned was forced to issue a grovelling apology, and pay tens of thousands of pounds in damages.

A small number of UKIP candidates did or said bad things (as happens to any political party ever), but these were making front-page news. Nigel Farage, in particular, insisted upon ruthlessness.

Better to suspend and expel a few people, than let the general public think that's the nature of the Party. Those actions were enough to prevent entryism, at that time, from taking the Party in a different direction.

In May 2013, UKIP was taking seats across the country and becoming the official opposition on many Councils, taking 1.25 million votes in the process. The word UKIP was trending on Twitter worldwide. When UKIP continued in similar vein, winning the 2014 European elections and winning Council elections and by-elections along the way, it reached a critical mass. It jumped - for a General Election - to around 20% in the opinion polls. That would easily have been enough to win seats, probably in substantial numbers.

UKIP's professionalism increased. It learned how to campaign, how to canvass, how to use the data gleaned, how to target messaging at particular areas. It started to grow up as a Party. Two Conservative MPs, Douglas Carswell and Mark Reckless, defected to it. They held by-elections; they were both re-elected. Had the Party truly realised the chance it had in another by-election on the same day as Clacton, it might well have gained a third MP in John Bickley. UKIP came within 632 votes of winning in a traditional Labour seat, Heywood and Middleton. Future historians, if they ever drill down deeply enough, will find half a dozen moments at least - including this one - where UKIP could, with different decisions, have gone on to be a huge Westminster force, potentially even to become a government.

But for the 2015 General Election, the Party suffered from a little vertigo. Having gained so much support, riding high in the polls, it feared that it would be squeezed during a General Election campaign. Sadly, resorting to a core-vote strategy, it focused almost exclusively on the issues of the EU and immigration - despite having a comprehensive, fully-costed Manifesto and the ability to fight on an even footing with the biggest parties.

It finished with 12.6% of the vote, more than the Liberal Democrats, but with just one MP. The fall from 20% in opinion polls at the turn of the year had been a steep and rapid one. UKIP would never be quite the same political force again.

UKIP had gone from too much focus on just the European Union - and, if forced to talk about something else, that would be immigration - to a broader-based Party, and back again. What happened in the middle had truly transformed British politics.

It had, though, achieved one lasting legacy. It forced, in early 2013, David Cameron to pledge an In/Out EU referendum if he won the next election. Perhaps he didn't expect at that point to be able to follow through on the pledge, being behind in most opinion polls. Few people truly saw the Conservatives' overall majority in 2015 coming. That UKIP was still a major force by the 2015 General Election ensured that David Cameron could not remove that pledge from the Manifesto if he wanted to.

It led to a serious irony. Tony Blair and David Cameron were, in one sense, the two people most responsible for the situation in which we ended up having a referendum. It would be hard to find two people more committed to staying in the European Union, but between them their actions created the conditions for a Brexit vote.

The UKIP surge wasn't about immigration, but the conditions for the UKIP surge were caused by immigration.

Could Brexit have happened without immigration issues? Probably not - but then again, you could say exactly the same about other facets of the European Union.

If the UK weren't a net contributor to the EU budget, would the Brexit vote still have happened? Probably not.

If the EU were not able to overrule UK law, would the Brexit vote still have happened? Probably not.

Despite that, there's something specific about immigration: it was an undercurrent that precipitated the seismic shifts in British politics that led to the referendum in the first place. It was then a huge factor during that referendum campaign.

Was immigration the reason for Brexit? Immigration was an issue. It was one of the most important issues. It was, arguably, the most important issue. But it was not the only issue.

CHAPTER 4

IS IT TRUE THAT ONE SIDE LIED IN THE REFERENDUM?

The whole basis of politics since 2016 has been, essentially, a fight between three camps:

1) Those who voted Leave and support the implementation of the referendum result

2) Those who voted Remain, but still believe that the result of the referendum must be respected - and that therefore, the UK must leave the European Union

3) Those who voted Remain, and seek to overturn the referendum result to ensure that the UK remains in the European Union

For the group in 3), there are essentially only two or three arguments that they can make. They can say that we now know things which we didn't know before about what Brexit can mean. They can say that they believe leaving the EU to be so bad, that they would rather overturn a referendum result than to accept it. The other option, and by far and away the one which would - if proven - provide them with the most democratic legitimacy to back up their actions, is to attempt to demonstrate that the outcome of the referendum was in some way unfair.

This argument, in one way or another, usually boils down to a claim that the Leave campaign lied to voters. Before this, let's take a quick look at the other claims that tend to be made from time to time.

Claim: That Leave broke the Electoral Commission's rules in terms of funding, giving them an unfair advantage.

The difficulty with making this case is that Remain spent far more money than Leave did during the campaign.

Remain spending: £19.1 million
Leave spending: £13.4 million

For every £2 spent by Leave, £3 was spent by Remain. Worse than that, the cost of government publicity including a leaflet to every house recommending a Remain vote was slightly more than £9 million.

If you count the government publicity in the totals, then Remain outspent Leave by 2:1. If you don't count it, then Remain still outspent Leave by a 3:2 margin. It would be easier for Remain to appeal to someone's general sense of fairness if this were not the case.

This led to quotes like this one by Tim Shipman, the political editor of the Sunday Times: "*The Remain campaign coordinated their efforts on a conference call every morning. They used taxpayers' money to send campaign literature to every household under the guise of information. If it was stacked, it was stacked against Leave. I voted Remain but this is ridiculous.*"

So what exactly is the claim that money was misused? Well, official Leave and Remain campaigns had spending limits. Other campaigns were permitted, and could be registered, but they had lower spending limits. What was not permitted, is co-ordination between the official campaign and non-official campaigns. If you're not part of the same campaign, you're not supposed to work together in a way that could make it look that you were trying to get around the spending limits.

The problem is that in practice, campaigns have to listen to what the Electoral Commission tells them. And, in a High Court judgement, the court ruled that the Electoral Commission had misinterpreted official guidance. The Electoral Commission fined the official Leave campaign, after the official Leave campaign essentially followed its advice.

They also fined Remain campaigns, including the Britain Stronger in Europe campaign and the Liberal Democrats.

Given changes to the rules surrounding referendums, and given that campaigns essentially set up from nothing over a short period of time rather than having decades' knowledge of accumulated understanding of arcane spending law, it's not particularly surprising that there were allegations made against both Leave and Remain. It's not particularly surprising either that some complaints were upheld.

The influential blogger claimed that "The Remain campaign did exactly the same thing as Vote Leave, only with more money and with five new campaigns."

The whole thing only gets more messy; allegations fly about from side to side. Remain campaigners accuse Vote Leave and Leave.EU of having flouted the law; Leave campaigners accuse the Electoral Commission of bias because similar accusations against the Remain campaigns were exonerated - such claims being 'evidenced' by the number of members of the Electoral Commission who had worked for pro-EU organisations, or publicly expressed pro-EU views.

These accusations fly around from side to side, but ultimately it's a difficult ask for Remain campaigners to persuade the public that the referendum campaign was unfairly biased against Remain, when they (effectively) spent twice as much on the campaign as Leave did.

Claim: Russia influenced the EU referendum campaign

Here, again, Remain campaigners have a problem. The notion that Russia attempted to influence the campaign is one with very little evidence supporting it.

The strongest evidence supporting this is from Facebook itself, which reports that a group calling itself the Internet Research Agency - and which has links to the Russian government - may have paid for Facebook advertising.

The problem with that evidence? Well, the amount of money involved was just $0.97 - or just 73 pence, at the exchange rate used at the time. It seems, according to Facebook, that this 73 pence was spent mistakenly: "We have determined that these accounts associated with the IRA [Internet Research Agency] spent a small amount of money ($0.97) on advertisements that delivered to UK audiences during that time. This amount resulted in three advertisements (each of which were also targeted to US audiences and concerned immigration, not the EU referendum) delivering approximately 200 impressions to UK viewers over four days in May 2016."

So if a Russian-linked organisation did accidentally spend 73 pence in the UK on adverts aimed at American citizens concerning immigration, and I think it probably did, it's really a little silly to try to complain that this is evidence of systematic and deliberate Russian interference in the referendum.

Leave campaigners point out that, at the behest of David Cameron, the (then) U.S. President Barack Obama made public anti-Brexit comments in the referendum campaign - suggesting that Britain would go to the 'back of the queue' for a trade deal. The fact that Obama used the English word 'queue' rather than the American 'line' hinted that perhaps the comments had been written in the UK.

A former White House adviser, Ben Rhodes, suggests that it was UK government sources who asked him to use that line:

"We had come here to try to help the Remain campaign and we had a meeting with David Cameron and his team...we all were agreeing that [a quick UK-US free trade deal being negotiated] was unlikely to happen. As Obama was saying that, somebody on the British side said 'yes, we'd end up being back of the queue' and everyone laughed and Obama said 'that's exactly right'. Then he was asked 'well, it would be good if you could repeat that point in the press conference' and, of course, he did."

The Remain side have a plausibility problem with claiming outside interference in a referendum campaign: it is well-known, well-documented, and admitted that they did the same thing - on a much bigger scale.

We're back to the original question:

Did one side lie during the referendum campaign?

Discuss Brexit, and I'll bet you a euro to a cent that sooner or later someone will mention Vote Leave's bus which claimed post-Brexit we'd have an extra £350 million per week which could be spent on our NHS. Boris Johnson has repeated the phrase again, and reignited the whole row. Thanks a million, Boris. Or three hundred and fifty million, I suppose.

I was never totally keen on the use of the £350 million figure. During the campaign, I always put the figure in context as a gross one, and explained that the rebate and EU funding should be taken off. And to be fair to Vote Leave, they did put that figure into context elsewhere in their spending plans – but those spending plans weren't as widely circulated.

But what actually is the truth over £350 million per week? The picture fluctuates from year to year, with changes to each economy, the EU budget, and exchange rates. No figure will ever be perfect. The latest accurate data available is the Pink Book 2016 produced by the Office of National Statistics; the most impeccable source because it looks at what's actually been paid in the past, not estimates or projections in the future. It puts the EU contribution for the previous year at £19.593 billion (gross), which is roughly £376 million per week.

Out of that, though, the UK gets the famous 'rebate' (technically, Fontainebleau abatement) won by Thatcher: a recognition that the way the EU budget is calculated leaves the UK out of pocket. Our £4.913 billion rebate comes to around £94 million per week. Think of that as being instant cashback. Leave the EU, and we can't spend that money because we lose the cashback.

Out of that, the EU gives us some of our own money back in 'EU funding'. We've paid for it; indeed, some £9.24 billion is shown as credited to the UK's account (but nearly £5 billion of that is the rebate we've already accounted for).

We're almost done, I promise! The EU does, however, give some money directly to UK businesses et al – bypassing the UK account altogether. So, cross-referencing with the Commission's own figures and applying the average pound-euro exchange rate from 2015, we get a figure of about £102 million per week for EU money coming back to the UK.

So take a deep breath, and the picture for 2015 - the last year before the referendum - is actually very simple: we paid £376 million a week, which became £282 million a week after cashback. After all the 'benefits' of EU funding, there was £180 million left. Personally, I'd have preferred Vote Leave to just stick £180 million per week on the side of the bus. It wouldn't have altered the referendum result in the slightest, and we wouldn't be still having this discussion now, more than two years after the referendum. But what's done is done; as the tart-tongued Lady Olenna Tyrell famously said in Game of Thrones "Once the cow's been milked, there's no squirting the milk back up her udder so here we are".

There's a sting in the tail though. Whilst I'd have preferred a figure of £180 million per week, the £282 million per week 'post-cashback' figure is easily defended if put into context. And the Office for Budget Responsibility projects that figure will rise to £335 million per week by the end of this Parliament.

Would I have made the same claim as Vote Leave, in the same way? Would I have repeated it, as Boris Johnson did? No. Is it absolutely 100% watertight? No.

It's a similar situation when it comes to Turkey. It's an agreed fact that Turkey's negotiations to join the European Union began officially on October 3 2005. This has progressed slowly, but it has progressed: at the time of the referendum, 16 of the 35 necessary chapters had been opened, and one had been completed and closed. It's also certainly true that the European Union was giving substantial amounts of money to Turkey in what's known as 'pre-accession funding', money to help Turkey prepare to join the European Union. That's something I had raised, and questioned the European Commission on over a year before the referendum. It's also true that *if* Turkey had joined the European Union, **then** it would eventually be subject to all the same rules as the rest of the European Union - including the so-called 'free movement' which would entail unlimited immigration from a huge nation which at the time had a population of over 75 million people, and which as we move towards 2019 is on the point of surpassing 80 million.

The Leave campaigns were correct to point this out. That being said, they did imply that it was more imminent than they should have. It was clear, at least to me (and again, I said this during the referendum campaign) that Turkey wouldn't be joining the European Union within the next couple of years.

As it happens, since the referendum, the prospect of Turkey joining the European Union has diminished. The things that eurosceptics were saying for a while about the human rights situation in Turkey under Erdogan suddenly started to be picked up by the European political mainstream, who suddenly realised that the comments were actually real.

Back to my 'whopper scale' of 0-10, I'd place the Vote Leave claims about Turkey somewhere around a 3. They were based in fact, but there was something slightly misleading about it.

For full disclosure, there's a third part of the Leave campaign (this time Leave.EU rather than Vote Leave) that I wasn't keen on. Indeed, I think it cost Leave quite a lot of votes. There's a false memory of the referendum campaign: a lot of people want to say that 'the polls were wrong'. That's not entierely true. A week and a half before the referendum, some polls started to show Leave as much as 10% ahead of Remain. Then, one day changed the course of the campaign. The awful murder of Labour's Jo Cox MP, by Thomas Mair. Thomas Mair was probably a white supremacist; he had viewed neo-Nazi and white surpremacist websites, and researched the Ku Klux Klan. When he killed Jo Cox, the nation was in shock.

Such evil, just a week before the referendum, led to the suspension of official campaigning.

The timing couldn't have been worse for Leave: one of the unofficial Leave campaigns had just unleashed a new, hard-hitting advert which has come to be known as the 'Breaking Point' poster. It showed a large number of migrants, implicitly suggesting that they were attempting to get to Britain. Britain was at 'breaking point', and only leaving the EU could solve that. The problem with the poster was that it conflated legal 'free movement' with illegal crossing of borders.

It didn't go down well with Leave campaigners at the time either. Whilst Remain still uses this as a claim that Leave lied to voters, it's worth noting that this poster was disavowed by the official Leave campaign anyway. Michael Gove, for example, said "When I saw that poster I shuddered. I thought it was the wrong thing to do."

Without that poster, I suspect that Leave would have won by a slightly larger margin. Others would disagree with me. I understand that some people do credit it for the high turnout in the referendum, but I find that a stretch personally.

Over the course of the referendum campaign, there were certainly three seriously controversial messages. Each was based upon a truth, but each stretched it in a way.

The big question, though, is how the accuracy of Leave's campaign compares to the accuracy of Remain's. I still recall George Osborne's predictions from May 23rd, 2016 that a vote for Brexit would lower GDP and cost 800,000 jobs by 2018. At the time, Osborne was the Chancellor of the Exchequer. In fact, GDP has grown and unemployment is currently at its lowest level since 1975. The EU Council President said Brexit could end 'Western political civilisation as we know it' and David Cameron threatened that Brexit could lead to war in Europe. People were threatened by the Chancellor with what was dubbed a 'punishment budget' if they voted to Leave; they were told to brace themselves for an emergency increase in taxes: "There would have to be increases in tax and cuts in public spending to fill the black hole".

Needless to say, none of this actually happened. Other promises didn't materialise either (such as the promise that the Prime Minister wouldn't step down if he lost the referendum - that one was broken within hours of the result being known). This leads to a new sleight-of-hand trick. These claims were all that bad things would happen instantly to the economy in the event of a Leave vote. They weren't claims for what happens after the two-year period envisaged in Article 50. When those things didn't occur immediately, the claims mysteriously shifted. Now, the bad things were rescheduled for whatever date the UK actually ended up exiting the European Union.

I just don't see how anyone can realistically believe that the Leave campaign lied to the British public, without also concluding that the Remain campaign told more - and bigger - lies. It's part of the tribal mindset of modern politics. I might well get quite a bit of flak from Leave campaigners because I've pointed out that the Leave campaign wasn't perfect, earlier in this chapter. It's what happens in politics.

When continuity Remainers criticise the £350 million per week figure, they develop an instant selective amnesia: Biblical phrases about hypocrisy, and taking the plank out of your own eye before complaining about the speck in someone else's, spring to mind.

But when it comes to lies told in the referendum campaign, Remain certainly have a few whoppers of their own.

CHAPTER 5

ARTICLE 50 AND THE 1972 ACT

How could the United Kingdom leave the European Union? There were two possibilities. The first is simple and straightforward to understand. When the UK signed the Lisbon Treaty, there's a provision in there (called Article 50) that allows us to give a 2-year notice that we're intending to leave the European Union. Think of it like leaving rented accommodation: you give the amount of notice that's specified in the contract.

The other means is this: to enter the (then) Common Market in the first place, we had to do that by an Act of Parliament. The 1972 European Communities Act took the UK into the European Union. Under British law, no Parliament may legally bind its successor. All Treaties and Acts of Parliament are subject to that principle. So, if the UK wanted to, we could legally choose to unilaterally repeal the 1972 European Communities Act and leave instantly.

Here's where everything started to go wrong after the referendum...

Everybody expected Article 50 to be triggered by the UK immediately after the referendum result was announced. I was in the European Parliament on the day after the referendum. I was the representative of the EFDD Group in the European Parliament) at a behind-closed-doors meeting of the political group leaders known as the Conference of Presidents.

The meeting came as quite a shock for me; I'd never seen a reaction quite like what I saw from the President of the Parliament and the other political group leaders. The atmosphere was cold, frosty, with barely a veneer of politeness.

Martin Schulz, the President of the Parliament, was predictably angry whilst former Prime Minister of Belgium, Guy Verhofstadt, was a little more subdued than usual. There was an atmosphere of shock, as though they couldn't believe what had happened. The British people have spoken, said Schulz, and now they must hurry up and get on with it and be gone. Indeed, they were all adamant that Cameron should invoke Article 50 immediately.

The big television screens in the big Committee room played Cameron's resignation speech live, and they were all outraged that Cameron intended to allow his successor to invoke Article 50. Someone as pro-EU as Cameron couldn't bring himself to be the one to tell the EU formally that we're leaving.

The Parliament group leaders basically wanted the clock to begin ticking. They wanted to get on with the business of the European Union, and to get Brexit over with. They quite clearly felt snubbed by the result of the Brexit vote.

I found myself in a very difficult position: I wanted this to be done as soon as possible, but I supported the UK's legal right not to be dictated to by Brussels over timescales. Then, delay followed delay. The 1922 Committee, the committee of Conservative MPs which controls the process of a leadership election, proposed a timetable which would yield a new Prime Minister by September. But when the new Prime Minister, Theresa May, came into power, she didn't want to trigger Article 50 straight away. She wanted to ensure that she had a negotiating team in place, amongst other things. Then, there was a court case (more on that later in the book) brought by Gina Miller, seeking to force an Act of Parliament before Article 50 could be invoked.

Gina Miller won her court case, and legislation followed. The European Union (Notification of Withdrawal) Bill was passed, and Theresa May triggered Article 50 in late March 2017. Finally, after over nine months of waiting, it had been triggered.

In the meantime, though, all kinds of questions had arisen. We'll start by taking a quick look at what Article 50 actually says, because although it's pretty short, I'd bet that upwards of 90% of the population have never actually read it. It starts with this:

1. Any Member State may decide to withdraw from the Union in accordance with its own constitutional requirements.

This is pretty clear; it's for the UK to make its decision on how to leave. It's not for the European Union to tell us what our own constitutional requirements are.

2. A Member State which decides to withdraw shall notify the European Council of its intention. In the light of the guidelines provided by the European Council, the Union shall negotiate and conclude an agreement with that State, setting out the arrangements for its withdrawal, taking account of the framework for its future relationship with the Union. That agreement shall be negotiated in accordance with Article 218(3) of the Treaty on the Functioning of the European Union. It shall be concluded on behalf of the Union by the Council, acting by a qualified majority, after obtaining the consent of the European Parliament.

There's actually quite a lot to unpick from that. We should learn that:

1. The method of telling the EU that we're leaving is to notify the European Council. In the end, a traditional hand-delivered letter was considered to be the best way.

2. It's the European Council's job to negotiate an agreement with the UK.

3. The basis for negotiation is what's written in Article 218(3) of the TFEU - and that says: "The Commission, or the High Representative of the Union for Foreign Affairs and Security Policy where the agreement envisaged relates exclusively or principally to the common foreign and security policy, shall submit recommendations to the Council, which shall adopt a decision authorising the opening of negotiations and, depending on the subject of the agreement envisaged, nominating the Union negotiator or the head of the Union's negotiating team."

So, the European Commission has an involvement in the process too. In essence, the Council should set political priorities and the Commission should do the day-to-day negotiating, recommend who should be on the negotiating team, and so on.

4. The Council takes decisions by 'qualified majority'. This is defined in some detail, but it usually means a little more than half of all the countries, including some of the largest ones, have to agree. The key point though? It doesn't have to be unanimous. If one country disagrees, it can't torpedo the entire deal.

5. The deal requires the 'consent' of the European Parliament. That means that it has to be rubber-stamped, but the European Parliament has no power in principle other than that. As a courtesy, in fact, the European Parliament has been given more input in negotiations.

6. The European Parliament has to give its consent before the Council does.

Let's carry on with Article 50...

3. The Treaties shall cease to apply to the State in question from the date of entry into force of the withdrawal agreement or, failing that, two years after the notification referred to in paragraph 2, unless the European Council, in agreement with the Member State concerned, unanimously decides to extend this period.

Here, again, there are a few points which are worth being aware of:

1. The time limit is supposed to be two years. However, if the Withdrawal Agreement comes into force sooner, then that's okay.

2. If both sides want to extend that period, and take more than 2 years over negotiations, it's no longer just a 'qualified' majority that's needed. They'd have to agree - every single country in the EU27, and the UK as well of course.

3. If nothing else happens, and there's no Agreement, the UK simply leaves without a deal after the end of that two-year period.

As much as the language talks about an Agreement, and the possibility of less or more time being needed for that Agreement to be negotiated, the 'default position' is leaving without a deal after 2 years. That's what would happen if nobody could agree on anything - or if they all just sat on their hands.

4. For the purposes of paragraphs 2 and 3, the member of the European Council or of the Council representing the withdrawing Member State shall not participate in the discussions of the European Council or Council or in decisions concerning it.

That's actually pretty straightforward: we don't get to be part of the bits where the EU27 discuss how they're going to negotiate with us. We don't get a vote to count towards their qualified majority when they want to choose whether to approve or reject an Agreement.

And finally...

5. If a State which has withdrawn from the Union asks to rejoin, its request shall be subject to the procedure referred to in Article 49.

Article 49 talks about how a country can apply to join the EU. This clause just means that once we've left, we can't rejoin without going through the same process that any other country would have to. Fair enough.

So that's Article 50. The key is to remember that it sets a 2-year clock running. At the end of that 2-year clock we're out, unless something happens to change that. At the time of writing, the 2-year clock will end on March 29th 2019, at 11pm UK time (i.e. midnight on the Continent).

March 29th 2019 will be 2 years, 9 months and 6 days after the referendum. Many people who voted for Brexit are impatient about the length of time that this has taken. They also fear that the provisions of Article 50 to make the process take still longer could be triggered.

The frustration and delays caused by this (and the 2-year period) caused some people to call for the other legal route to leave the European Union to be used: repeal of the 1972 European Communities Act. As I said earlier in the chapter, under a long-established principle in British law, no Parliament may legally bind its successor. The 1972 European Communities Act enables the UK to be part of the EU. A future Parliament may not be bound by that decision, and therefore has the power to repeal that legislation and leave the Union.

Indeed, this idea became official UKIP policy shortly after the referendum, at the behest of Gerard Batten. I believe that this was two separate kinds of mistakes at the same time: it was *a political mistake*, and it was *wrong for the UK*.

Why do you say it was a political mistake?

It was a political mistake because it failed to understand the nature of the media. By going down that route, UKIP completely lost the ability to say anything on Brexit. When something happened in negotiations, the media would only be interested in a comment on what had just changed. If it's not new, it's not news! If your comment is always 'we shouldn't be doing this, we should be unilaterally repealing the 1972 Act instead', then sooner or later you're not going to be asked to provide comments. You can't say the same thing over and over again for two years, hoping that the media will want to print or broadcast it.

Why do you say it was wrong for the UK?

There's a saying; a threat is stronger than its execution. The idea of unilaterally withdrawing is a nuclear option.

All the Remain threats - 'what if there are tariffs', 'what happens about X, Y and Z where we need to co-operate with our neighbours' - would have had some meaning if we had left instantly without a plan. Well, not all their threats. We still wouldn't have World War 3 or the end of Western political civilisation as we know it, but it would be a shock to the economy. A more pertinent problem is this: could you imagine both Houses of Parliament unilaterally repealing the Act? I certainly couldn't at the time, and I still can't now. If Parliament won't do it, then whether you like it or not we're stuck with Article 50.

There was a better way though: to use Article 50, but keep the unilateral repeal as a 'nuclear option' which we could use if absolutely necessary.

At the end of July 2017, I wrote my regular column in the Newcastle Journal about how we should be approaching negotiations. The key point to note is that - even if we leave with no deal - we should have been busy negotiating trade deals with countries across the world. That way, the European Union would know that we're ready to do business with the world. Knowing that we weren't desperate for a deal, it would be easier for us to negotiate a good one.

I wanted us to be looking to the globe, not just to Europe. In my article, I wrote:

The European Union claims that under Article 4(3) of the Treaty on European Union, we can't do it. That gives us a duty of 'sincere co-operation' with the European Union whilst we're members of it. It's a great argument with just one small flaw: it's utter baloney. My apologies for getting technical for a moment, but whatever 'sincere co-operation' means, it cuts both ways. The EU isn't 'sincerely co-operating' with us if they deliberately try to make it harder for us to succeed post-Brexit. They're not meeting their obligations to their neighbours (ie. us) under Article 8 of the Lisbon Treaty either. And 'sincere co-operation' is poorly defined: it couldn't possibly take precedence over better-defined parts of the Treaty on European Union – like for example Article 21(2)(e) which speaks of "progressive abolition of restrictions on international trade". A European Union telling us we can't talk to other countries about the progressive abolition of restrictions on international trade is a European Union ignoring its own rules, which to be honest is one of the main reasons we're leaving in the first place. The European Union is supposed to respect the General Agreement on Tariffs and Trade 1994, of which Article 24(4) says that a Customs Union is to facilitate trade and not "to raise barriers to the trade of other contracting parties with such territories". Which is precisely what the EU is doing – not because of the UK, but because they're making it harder for Japan to negotiate a free trade deal with us by putting barriers in their way.

So the British government needs to get on with it, rather than playing into the EU's hands. We know the EU takes a decade or more, on average, to negotiate trade deals (and if the EU suddenly develops uncharacteristic speed and negotiates the deal before Brexit, grandfathering arrangements will then apply to the UK). It's a hugely bureaucratic process – not least because they need to get 28 countries to all agree a common negotiating position to be able to start negotiations with the other side. At every stage those 28 countries need to accept the deal, and any concessions made will disproportionately harm certain countries. But we can do better than a decade. If our government has the bottle, we can get there first. If the Philippines can negotiate a deal with EFTA in just one year, surely the UK can negotiate deals quickly too.

What's needed is the political will to make it happen. And that, with this Conservative government, is the biggest weakness in the whole Brexit process. Get Brexit right, and the benefits will be pretty much instant. Get it wrong, and it could take years. Courage seems to be in short supply at present: our government needs to develop a backbone – not just for the sake of workers in Sunderland, but for the many jobs that could be created if only it lost its self of self-deprecation and remembered that we're a world leader in research, intelligence, science and technology, that we speak a global language and that we're one of the world's largest economies.

This option - of using the Article 50 time to properly prepare ourselves for Brexit - seems to have been pretty much ignored. The level of planning and preparation for 'no deal' has been woefully insufficient from the start.

CHAPTER 6

WHY SHOULD THE REFERENDUM RESULT BE ACCEPTED?

A while ago, Sky News interviewed a lady called Liz Pugh, from Burnley, who worked in a fish and chip shop. She was asked what she thought would happen if we ended up with a so-called 'soft Brexit', or even no Brexit at all.

I'm mentioning this not because I agree with her, but because this is the level of concern being expressed by people - not people hiding behind a computer screen, somewhere on the internet - but something that she's prepared to say on television, to the nation:

Oh, there'll be mass riots. There'll be hysteria. There could even be a civil war to be fair with you. The country has used its voice and if the Government ignores what the people have said then there is going to be a civil war. There is going to be. They want to see what the government do next, that's what they want."

Interviewer: They keep talking about hard Brexit, soft Brexit. What if it isn't the full thing?

"Then I think a lot of people are gonna be extremely angry and let down. They're gonna be let down by their own government. Because people have spoken and if people don't get what they've asked for then people are gonna rise and people are gonna use their voice in different ways and they are gonna be angry, because I know I would

56

be."

We are, whether we like it or not, living in a divided nation. Anand Menon, a Professor of European Politics and Current Affairs at King's College London, wrote in the Guardian that we must:

Leave aside the questions as to what a reversal will do to trust in government and politics in general among leave voters. Leavers would not simply accept the result and give up. Rather, we would confront something akin to a political groundhog day.

It's not hard to find polemics by Remain supporters, often university academics, saying the same thing: that the consequences of overturning the referendum result would be severe in terms of the nation's future.

Would there really be such civil unrest in the UK if Brexit were to be overturned, or if the UK were bounced into such a situation? I don't think anyone really knows - but just look at what's happened in France recently, with the 'Gilet Jaune' protests. The argument against is simple, and plausible: the UK simply doesn't have a tradition of taking to the streets in the same way that France does, when there's a feeling that politicians have let the country down.

17.4 million people voted for Brexit. That doesn't mean that all 17.4 million consider it to be so important that it must overrule all else, or that democracy is dead if Brexit is not delivered. Nobody would expect 17.4 million people to all take to the streets at once. Having said that, it would be wrong to underestimate the possibility that there could be mass demonstrations in such an event.

I don't believe that the government should take that into account, as it happens. I don't believe that fear of mob rule should be a rationale for taking action.

What I do believe, is that there would be a legitimate grievance which would have long-term social consequences and scar our nation for a generation - at least. To see why, let's look at what people who strongly support Brexit have done:

1. In 2014, they elected a pro-Brexit political party in the European elections. It was the first time for over a century that any party other than Labour or the Conservatives had won any national elections.

2. In 2015, they elected a government on a specific Manifesto commitment of granting a referendum on leaving the European Union. The third-placed party in terms of vote share at that election simply wanted to leave the European Union, without a referendum.

(It's worth noting that the Lib Dems, when pledging an In/Out referendum in 2010, had a record result - then collapsed in 2015 when they'd reneged on that pledge. That may have something to do with Brexit, but the main causes were other things)

3. In 2016, more people voted for Brexit than have ever - in British political history - voted for anything at all. Nothing in the UK, at all, has a mandate that's been given by more than 17.4 million people - except for Brexit.

4. In 2017, at another General Election, over 84% of the vote went to partics pledging that they would respect, and implement, the referendum result.

After voting *four times* for Brexit, and winning every single time, people who support Brexit might well be thinking that they cannot do anything more. If Brexit were overturned now, what democratic recourse could they possibly have?

When I speak to people, the number of times I hear phrases like 'I don't see why I should ever bother to vote, ever again, because nothing ever changes', 'politicians are betraying us', or worse things that I really shouldn't repeat, tells me that there's something deeply wrong. I'm not just hearing those phrases from people who've held to extreme views in the past. I'm hearing it from people who are relatively moderate, but absolutely despairing because they believe that their very democracy is being stolen away from them.

Now, I don't believe that there are 17.4 million people in the country who would feel quite so passionately about it as that. I suspect, but of course can't prove, that we'd be talking something in the region of 5 to 6 million people who would feel that way.

Those people will continue to do everything that they can by democratic means, so long as they believe that there exists a reasoned democratic way of achieving their goals.

This is where there's a huge danger with the notion of a 'second referendum'. Not only was the referendum in 2016 billed as a 'once in a lifetime decision', and publicised as being such by the leading Remain campaigners out of fear that some would use it as a protest vote, but that referendum was held in the context of a political development involving three other elections, and two Acts of Parliament - as well as a Supreme Court case. But the legal issues around a hypothetical second referendum are for discussion in a later chapter.

CHAPTER 7

THE COURT CASES AND THEIR CONSEQUENCES

This is going to be the most technical chapter in the book. I'll try to keep it as simple as straightforward as possible, but if you want to truly understand Brexit then understanding the two most important court cases (and their implications) is absolutely essential.

On January 24, 2017, the UK Supreme Court ruled that the British government did not have the authority to give notice that it was triggering Article 50. That would have to be done by an Act of Parliament, rather than through what is commonly known as the 'Royal Prerogative'.

The Royal Prerogative, centuries ago, was the personal power of the King or Queen ruling the country at the time. They might sign Treaties, declare war upon their enemies, recognise foreign states, grant honours, aprove the appointment of bishops, hire and fire government ministers, or do many other things.

As time went on, this Royal Prerogative became more technical than actual. Nobody would expect the Queen to unilaterally decide to declare war, for example.

Most people have heard of the U.S. Constitution. It's an important, if sometimes arcane, document that determines how the United States must be run. The U.K. doesn't have a written Constitution. For that reason, you might often hear it said that the UK doesn't have a Constitution. A better way of looking at it is to say that the UK has an *unwritten Constitution*: courts over centuries have interpreted the law, developing these principles in detail.

Today, the Cabinet Manual describes the principle of how the government, and Cabinet, exercises those powers with the consent of the monarch of the day: it defines the Royal Prerogative as *"the residual power inherent in the Sovereign, and now exercised mostly on the advice of the Prime Minister and Ministers of the Crown".*

It describes how the Royal Prerogative works as follows: *"The scope of the Royal Prerogative power, which is the residual power inherent in the Sovereign, has evolved over time. Originally the Royal Prerogative would only have been exercised by the reigning Sovereign. However, ministers now exercise the bulk of the prerogative powers, either in their own right or through the advice that they provide to the Sovereign, which he or she is constitutionally bound to follow. The Sovereign is, however, entitled to be informed and consulted, and to advise, encourage and warn ministers".*

Parliament doesn't have the power to interfere with the Royal Prerogative. So, for example, in 1999 a Labour MP tried to introduce a Bill to Parliament to require Parliament's support before the government could take the nation to war against Iraq. But because declarations of war fall under the Royal Prerogative, such legislation would interfere with the power of the Crown (or, in practice, with the power of the government). In effect, it would have been a power-grab: from the government (using the Royal Prerogative) to the

Parliament. Many people might well think that would be a good thing, but such power grabs need the side that's potentially losing the power to agree to it.

For the debate and any vote to happen, the Queen would have to agree (as advised by the government). Whilst technically the Queen retains the power to do all manner of things, by *convention*, the Queen does as the government of the day requests. The Blair government advised that consent should not be given. The matter was not debated, and that was the end of the matter. There's one word, though, that *should* define the way that the government and Parliament work together: *respect*.

You might, as I do, believe that the eventual invasion of Iraq in 2003 was a mistake. I do not believe that the country should take war lightly. There needs to be a clearly-defined reason for action (the shift from 'weapons of mass destruction' to 'terrorism' to 'it was to liberate the Iraqi people' was troubling, because it shifted the goalposts). There needs to be a clearly-defined military objective, and - most importantly - there needs to be a credible plan for what happens after that objective is achieved.

In the absence of those things, it's no surprise that Iraq descended into chaos. The rise of the terror organisation ISIS was facilitated, at least in part, by the vacuum created by our own actions in Iraq.

But whilst I believe the Iraq war was a mistake, I nonetheless recognise that Parliament was consulted on it. The government did not (thanks to the Royal Prerogative) have any requirement to consult Parliament, but it chose to consult Parliament anyway. The motion was passed comfortably, with both Labour and Conservatives supporting it despite backbench rebellions on both sides.

Morally, Parliament had been consulted on the triggering of Article 50. The fact that an Act of Parliament had authorised a referendum on EU withdrawal should, according to common sense, be sufficient for the government to act on that basis and trigger Article 50.

There's a difference, though, between legally and morally. The question asked of the Supreme Court was (effectively) this: Can the government use the Royal Prerogative to trigger Article 50, or does it require a completely separate piece of legislation?

At the time, Remain campaigners hoped that separate legislation would be required. That was the basis of the legal challenge. Leave campaigners thought that the referendum was sufficient.

The argument advanced by Gina Miller, and those suggesting that Parliament should have to pass a separate Bill in order to trigger Article 50, was basically as follows:

1. Triggering Article 50 would - in effect - force Acts of Parliament to be repealed: the 1972 European Communities Act, the Single European Act, and so on. The Royal Prerogative doesn't extend to overruling primary legislation.

2. The Royal Prerogative might cover a Treaty in general, but it shouldn't cover the 1972 European Communities Act because that was constitutional in nature. The 1972 European Communities Act isn't just an ordinary Act of Parliament, because of its constitutional nature.

3. Once given, notice under Article 50 cannot be withdrawn - the decision is irreversible.

Whilst government ministers had promised that they would be putting further legislation before Parliament - the so-called Great Repeal Bill - the Supreme Court decided that it couldn't consider government promises. Indeed, in the judgement, the Supreme Court said *"As was made clear by Lord Browne-Wilkinson in R v Secretary of State for the Home Department, Ex p Fire Brigades Union [1995] 2 AC 513, 552, ministers' intentions are not law".*

Lord Pannick QC described the Royal Prerogative in terms of firing a gun: when you pull the trigger, it causes the bullet to be fired. The consequence of that firing is that the bullet will hit the target - in this case, that Treaties will no longer apply. In his view, that would basically pre-empt the role of Parliament.

Court judgements going back to the 17th century were quoted in the Supreme Court: the Case of Proclamations in 1610 had said that "the King by his proclamation or other ways cannot change any part of the common law, or statute law, or the customs of the realm". In our modern society, the word 'King' might be substituted for 'government' - but the principle still applies.

The Attorney General supported the UK government's position on

Article 50 - namely, that it could be triggered by Royal Prerogative. He effectively argued that yes, the 1972 Act does give power to EU law - but only insofar as the EU Treaties require it. Signing or withdrawing from a Treaty has traditionally been part of the Royal Prerogative.

The Supreme Court was eventually convinced by Lord Pannick's argument. It determined that this would require a change in the law - and therefore, an Act of Parliament would be required: *"Where, as in this case, implementation of a referendum result requires a change in the law of the land, and statute has not provided for that change, the change in the law must be made in the only way in which the UK constitution permits, namely through Parliamentary legislation".*

The Supreme Court judgement describes the referendum as of 'great political significance', but that its force is political rather than legal until such time as it is written into law.

So why does all this matter? Parliament legislated fairly quickly: the European Union (Notification of Withdrawal) Act 2017 said that *"The Prime Minister may notify, under Article 50(2) of the Treaty on European Union, the United Kingdom's intention to withdraw from the EU. This section has effect despite any provision made by or under the European Communities Act 1972 or any other enactment.."*

Legislation in the UK is normally long, and complicated. This was not: it was as straightforward as any legislation that Parliament has passed in my lifetime. Other than the title, I've quoted the full thing here. It's just 42 words; the shortest ever Act of Parliament is the

Parliament (Qualification of Women) Act 1918 which ensured that women could sit as Members of Parliament.

The more substantial legislation was left until 2018, for the European Union (Withdrawal) Act 2018. Again, this gets complicated - but the legislation is designed to give Parliament control over parts of the process. Section 13 of that Act is all about the so-called 'meaningful vote' which has to take place in Parliament.

The wording requires Ministers to make a statement to Parliament, setting out their intentions if one of three things happens:

- If Parliament rejects the deal
- If agreement can't be reached with the EU
- If there is no deal by 21 January 2019

The legislation also means that the government cannot ratify the deal unless Parliament has first approved the deal.

It also sets out four conditions for the Withdrawal Agreement. That can only be ratified if:

- A Minister has laid the relevant documents before Parliament and made a statement to state that agreement has been reached
- The Commons approves the Agreement
- The Lords has had chance to debate the Agreement
- An Act of Parliament has been passed which contains provision for implementing the Agreement

The deadline of January 21st is the deadline for responding to an inability to agree a deal. It's nothing to do with what happens, at least in law, if a deal has been reached. Holding the meaningful vote on March 28th would comply with the letter of the law, if not the spirit.

Between the Iraq War and today, there's been another legislative change. The Constitutional Reform and Governance Act 2010 requires the government to lay before Parliament any Treaties it wishes to ratify, at least 21 sitting days before the Treaty is ratified. Parliament can 'reset the clock' by voting to ensure that the Treaty cannot be ratified. Theoretically, they could do this at least once every 21 days and block the government's power to ratify a Treaty.

On a legal basis, there's a lot that needs to happen - even if the House of Commons does approve the Withdrawal Agreement. This is the reason why Jeremy Corbyn accused Theresa May of 'running down the clock' in Prime Minister's Questions on December 19th 2018. Knowing that the government didn't plan to hold the meaningful vote until the week commencing January 14th, that would leave barely ten weeks for all the Parliamentary processes. Supposing that Parliament votes down that deal, time is even shorter.

The effect of such running down the clock is to make alternative options more difficult. Even negotiating a simple free trade deal isn't something that's very quick to achieve, so the impact of Theresa May's strategy is to try to reduce the number of available options to three. That's actually pretty close to what she told the radio station LBC before the original vote was delayed. The media reported it as 'my deal, no deal, or no Brexit'. May's actual words were "There are three options: one is to leave the European Union with a deal... the other two are that we leave without a deal or that we have no Brexit at all".

Taking away options like the Canada option, the 'Norway to Canada' option, and even the options which Jeremy Corbyn might prefer - such as a straightforward Norway-style deal - is a strategy which you might not like, but it's one which is fairly effective in cynical game-theoretic terms. Theresa May effectively gambled that, by running down the clock, the alternative options would be hard to agree.

This leads us on to the second court case: is Remain even a legal option at this stage? Article 50 contains no provision by which it could possibly be overturned.

Here is where, sadly, one huge mistake was made by UKIP in April 2018. The official statement by Gerard Batten, after a vote by the House of Lords, was: "Lord Kerr was the man who drafted Article 50 in such a way that EU exit can be delayed, impeded and overturned. Acting true to form he is now trying to carry it through to its purpose. UKIP will continue to fight for a complete and clean exit from the EU."

This was a mistake, because it conceded a fundamental legal point to those advocating for Remain. The fact was (at the time) that there was no mechanism by which Article 50 could be revoked: this removed any possibility of being able to argue otherwise at a later date. Two Scottish MEPs (David Martin, Labour and Alyn Smyth,

SNP), together with MSPs Andy Wightman and Ross Greer (Green), embarked on a legal challenge against this, suggesting that the UK must be free to revoke its notification if it wishes. The matter was headed back to court. The Scottish Court of Session decided, after an appeal, to refer the matter, using an urgent process, to the Court of Justice of the European Union. They asked the Court to rule on the following question:

Where, in accordance with Article 50 of the TEU, a Member State has notified the European Council of its intention to withdraw from the European Union, does EU law permit that notice to be revoked unilaterally by the notifying Member State; and, if so, subject to what conditions and with what effect relative to the Member State remaining within the EU?

The British Government and the European Union seemed to be on the same side of this question, but for very different reasons.

The British Government did not want political pressure to be placed upon them to reverse Brexit. The Gina Miller court case was based upon Article 50 being irreversible. *Their position: Article 50 could not be unilaterally revoked.*

The European Union was worried that, if Article 50 could be unilaterally revoked, that countries could trigger Article 50 as a negotiating ploy. They could, once receiving concessions they want, say 'Okay, we'll stay after all'. That could cause chaos. *Their position: Article 50 could not be unilaterally revoked.*

The Court ruled in favour of the Scottish politicians, and against both the UK Government and the European Union's position.

One common misunderstanding amongst British eurosceptics was that the European Union would be delighted by this result. It wasn't. There was also an accusation made that the timing of the judgement was political: namely, that the process had been done so quickly as to torpedo Theresa May's so-called 'meaningful vote'. This was perhaps slightly unfair as a claim. If courts considered it to be an important legal issue, then it would need to be resolved quickly.

What was missed, in all of this, was a far more serious charge: for the first time, in such a serious case, *the European Court of Justice was itself writing the law*. This notion, often known as 'judicial activism', is common in the United States of America.

The European Court of Justice has always interpreted the law, to an extent, in a way that develops understanding of the law. This goes all the way back to 1979, to the *Cassis de Dijon case*. There's an expansionist approach to interpreting the law, though, and there's rewriting the law as a whole.

In this case, to say that Article 50 could be revoked just as easily as it could be revoked, the Court went far further than it had ever done in the past.

This has a few key implications for Brexit, some obvious and others not quite so obvious:

1. The UK Government could technically now reverse its Article 50 notification...in accordance with its own constitutional requirements.

Remember that phrase? It's taken directly from Article 50...and the Gina Miller case found that this required an Act of Parliament. If the Government doesn't have the power to invoke Article 50 'in accordance with its own constitutional requirements' without an Act of Parliament, how could it possibly revoke Article 50 'in accordance with its own constitutional requirements' without an Act of Parliament?

Gina Miller's court case could, ironically, turn out to ensure that the UK does, in fact, leave the European Union. To do anything other than leave would require further legislation.

Gavin Phillipson (Professor of Law at Durham University) and Alison Young (Sir David Williams Professor of Public Law, Robinson College, University of Cambridge), argue that this is the case. Their claim (and I am trying to reflect pages of legal argument in a single sentence) is basically that the principle established in the Gina Miller case means that the Royal Prerogative can't be used to frustrate the will of Parliament; otherwise, we'd be back to the idea that the Prime Minister and Cabinet can overrule an Act of Parliament. The phrase 'will of Parliament' in this case means what Parliament has agreed in actual legislation.

There are other legal arguments, but I don't find them particularly persuasive. It would seem somewhat perverse to argue that the two are in any way different.

2. Under Theresa May's Withdrawal Agreement, even if the UK isn't technically required to refer cases to the ECJ, it's still got to 'have regard to' EU law. EU law is interpreted (naturally) by European Union courts. That interpretation (just like in the Cassis de Dijon case) is the issue. The more judicial power the ECJ has, the greater the risk under the Withdrawal Agreement.

3. The judgement suggests that we can't revoke, and then re-trigger, Article 50. It can't be used as a delaying tactic.

Do the court cases make Remain more, or less, likely? They were certainly designed to help Remain, but I'm not sure whether they actually do.

CHAPTER 8

THE NORTHERN IRELAND QUESTION

If you'd asked me before the referendum in 2016 (and some people did), I'd have said 'What Northern Ireland question?'. Look at it logically:

- The Republic of Ireland and Northern Ireland have had a Common Travel Area, allowing people to pass freely in either direction since 1923.
- The UK government does not want a hard border between Northern Ireland and the Republic of Ireland
- The people of Northern Ireland does not want a hard border between Northern Ireland and the Republic of Ireland
- The Republic of Ireland has stated that it will not impose a hard border between Northern Ireland and the Republic of Ireland
- The European Union states that it does not want to see a hard border between Northern Ireland and the Republic of Ireland
- The World Trade Organisation has stated that there is no requirement to impose a hard border

So, why are we even discussing this? It took me quite a while after the referendum result to realise that anyone was actually being serious about this.

Politicians have an annoying habit of using smoke-and-mirrors distraction tactics, creating issues where no issues actually exist, in order to push a particular agenda. I rather naively assumed that, because absolutely nobody wanted to introduce a new border, such issues would easily be resolved.

So why are we even having this conversation? Well, essentially the whole thing is a tussle about UK policy. Take a few of these post-Brexit scenarios. Some of them will appeal to people in the UK, but they very much don't appeal to the European Union.

Scenario 1: Having left the Common Agricultural Policy, the UK provides more efficient subsidies for its own farmers. British farmers are able to grow cheaper food.

Scenario 2: The UK wants to increase its own competitiveness after Brexit. Therefore, it decides to cut Corporation Tax so that it has lower levels than anywhere in the European Union.

Scenario 3: After Brexit, the UK negotiates a free trade deal with India, enabling it to import cheaper goods so that British consumers benefit from lower prices.

Scenario 4: The UK decides that some EU standards don't serve any useful purpose. They decide that those standards will no longer be applicable post-Brexit, and that the UK will set its own business-friendly rules.

The European Union does not like any of these scenarios at all. Each of them would provide the UK with competitive advantages over the European Union. They might well result in the UK winning contracts which EU nations wanted to win, or in businesses choosing to move to the UK.

> 💡 **The number one thing that people fail to understand about the European Union is this: it's a protectionist organisation.**

We hear a lot in the media about protectionism at national level, referring to Donald Trump or the leaders of any of a number of countries.

The European Union is protectionist of its own interests. The Customs Union is precisely that: it's designed to protect goods within the Union, to the expense of goods from outside the Union.

So, how is the European Union going to react to Brexit in general? Well, in one sense it doesn't really mind that much if the UK leaves. Britain has often been out of kilter with other EU countries in the past. The EU can cope with the UK leaving. What it would find very difficult to cope with is:

1. If the UK were seen to prosper after leaving the EU, causing other EU nations to think of doing the same

2. If the UK were to act in any way which interferes with the European Union's protectionism

3. If Brexit were to cause any difficulties with the integrity of their own Customs Union

The whole Northern Ireland question needs to be seen in terms of the broader European Union's approach. Any of the four scenarios earlier in this chapter would cause the European Union a serious problem, but it can't really say so directly.

Suppose that the European Union were to say to the UK "*We're terrified that you're going to take our business post-Brexit by making your economy more competitive*". What would the UK's response be? I'm guessing that it would be something similar to "*Get your nose out of our business*", but in more diplomatic language.

The European Union's Customs Union requires goods to be able to move freely within the Customs Union. Once a good has found its way into the European Union, it needs to be able to be traded freely within the EU without any further problems.

What if, instead, the European Union were to say this to the UK?

"*We're worried that if you make these changes to your goods, those goods will cross the border into the Republic of Ireland, and this will undermine the integrity of the Customs Union.*"

Furthermore, they could start to talk about supply chains. Suppose that the UK produced a car engine, which was then exported to the Republic of Ireland and used to manufacture a car. That car was then sold to France. In this case, 'goods' which may not meet the European Union's standards - or, indeed, be entitled to be in the European Union in the first place. By making arguments like this, the European Union can give legitimacy to the arguments it would *like* to make (but can't) about stopping the United Kingdom from prospering outside the European Union by taking its business.

A hard border in Northern Ireland would solve the technical problem for the European Union. With border posts and customs checks on goods coming in and out, there would be no need to worry about the integrity of the European Union's territory (*note: the EU thinks about 'its territory' in the same kind of way that a nation state would typically think about its territory*).

But the European Union didn't want to force a hard border on Northern Ireland; politically that would be a bad thing. Worse still, this situation wouldn't resolve their actual concern: that a low-tax, low-regulation, English-speaking economic powerhouse on its external border would take business from it.

Therefore, the European Union sought to mitigate this threat by ensuring that there is no hard border in Northern Ireland. By stipulating that there must be no hard border, the European Union can then attempt to further stipulate that the United Kingdom must agree in the Withdrawal Agreement not to do anything which might undermine the integrity of the Customs Union.

The UK must, under such an arrangement, agree to all kinds of things to prevent the distortion of European markets. In so doing, the UK will then be unable to demonstrate any significant competitive advantage over the European Union's own policies.

For the United Kingdom, the desire to avoid a hard border in Northern Ireland is much more a matter of principle. Nobody wants to risk the peace process, or the Good Friday Agreement. They wouldn't want to be the ones to insist upon border posts.

The European Union responded, in effect, by doing the polar opposite of the famous line from the Godfather: by *making the UK an offer it couldn't accept.* They suggested that *if* Northern Ireland were to remain in the Customs Union and the Single Market, *then* the rest of the UK could have the kind of free trade deal it wanted.

This non-offer was clearly a non-offer, because it would mean that the rest of the UK would have a different regime to Northern Ireland. The UK would then be forced to maintain its own hard border between England/Scotland/Wales and Northern Ireland. Having established this principle, doubtless Scotland would then demand the same. The European Union's offer was a subtle attempt at divide-and-conquer.

Meanwhile, Sinn Fein and others who wished to see Northern Ireland subsumed into the Republic of Ireland to become a 'united Ireland', as they describe it, were only too delighted at the prospect of a border in the Irish Sea. This would cause convergence between Northern Ireland and the Republic, whilst simultaneously causing divergence between Northern Ireland and the rest of the UK.

Therefore, there was significant political pressure to insist upon a resolution to the Northern Ireland question. All of this suited the Republic of Ireland's political interests, for the same reasons as it suited the European Union's - but with even more at stake. The Republic of Ireland has some of the lowest rates of Corporation Tax in the European Union. It's also an English-speaking nation. Google maintains its European headquarters in Dublin, and describes it as the 'data capital of Europe'. The worst thing that could happen to Dublin is if the UK were to take business away from it. Therefore, the Republic of Ireland's own interests were served by falling into line with the European Union's own position.

The stage was set for the Northern Ireland border to become a proxy war in Brexit negotiations.

In the United Kingdom, this was treated as being a practical problem rather than a political one. The UK tried to work with the Irish Taoiseach [Prime Minister] Enda Kenny to try to find a practical solution.

The principles were:

1. There really aren't that many goods crossing the border from Northern Ireland to the Republic of Ireland.

2. Modern technology has come a long way: there are means of ensuring that goods can be tracked.

3. There are only a few routes across the border; it would easily be possible to install cameras, possibly not even at the border itself, to ensure that monitoring could occur without having to install actual border posts.

The UK started looking at Authorised Economic Operator schemes, similar to the principles it already uses for imports and exports customs checks at the moment.

The government website describes it as "an internationally recognised quality mark that shows your role in the international supply chain is secure", and that your "customs controls and procedures are efficient and meet EU standards". They say "It's not mandatory, but gives quicker access to some simplified customs procedures and, in some cases, the right to 'fast-track' your shipments through some customs and safety and security procedures."

So far, so good. Negotiations seemed to be going reasonably well on that front. Then, in May 2017, Enda Kenny resigned. The leadership contest was somewhat reminiscent of Labour's 'which Miliband?' problem, which they'd answered incorrectly in 2010. Whilst Simon Coveney won most votes, under the electoral college system used, Leo Varadkar won the contest.

The new Taoiseach had a point to prove. He needed to shore up his position with his own party membership. Varadkar could kill two birds with one stone: by being tough with the United Kingdom, he could help Brussels out - and be seen as someone standing up for Irish interests back at home.

The position of the Irish government changed, almost overnight. Tax officials in the Republic of Ireland went from believing that these problems could easily be solved to believing that they could not.

The European Union began to talk about a 'backstop' - the principle that Northern Ireland would have to remain in the Customs Union until or unless a workable solution could be found to this question of the Northern Ireland border.

This, of course, had consequences. Just a couple of months before Leo Varadkar became Taoiseach, Theresa May had called a General Election on the issue of Brexit - then spectacularly mismanaged the campaign, losing her overall majority.

Theresa May now had to rely upon the support of the Democratic Unionist Party (DUP)'s 10 Northern Irish seats in the House of Commons to be able to continue to command a majority in Parliament.

The DUP told Theresa May in no uncertain terms that she would not be continuing as Prime Minister if she were to agree to different arrangements for Northern Ireland than for the rest of the United Kingdom. Theresa May could not agree to a unilateral backstop in Northern Ireland.

As with everything Brexit, A leads to B and then B leads to C.

The EU insisted on a backstop in Northern Ireland.

The DUP would not allow it to apply to Northern Ireland only.

Therefore, the UK government insisted it must apply to the whole of the UK.

From there, many other things followed - but this story is better told in more detail in the chapter on the final Withdrawal Agreement. The problem is that, whilst the issue isn't *entirely* confected, the problems could easily be solved if the political will were there. The political will simply isn't there. As Liam Halligan wrote in the Telegraph,

"Technological and other solutions can solve this problem. The existing largely virtual border already copes with different currencies, excise duties, VAT rates, income and corporation tax. There is no reason minor trading rule variations can't also be managed, variations which would be even smaller if the UK and EU got beyond this backstop nonsense and negotiated a free-trade agreement."

The whole thing became a game of political brinkmanship. Everyone had clearly stated that they wouldn't be introducing a hard border in Northern Ireland. Yet, by insisting on the backstop, there would be a significantly increased risk of a no-deal Brexit which would hit Ireland harder than any other country in the European Union.

Had the United Kingdom been prepared to follow through on Theresa May's *'No deal is better than a bad deal'* principle, they might well have killed off the backstop idea.

In the end, Varadkar's will was stronger than May's.

CHAPTER 9

HOW DOES THE EU VIEW BREXIT?

Remember when Margaret Thatcher famously (or infamously, depending on your point of view) said 'There's no such thing as society'? You'll without a doubt have heard that there's also no such thing as a free lunch, or bad publicity, or darkness, or coincidence, or whichever concept people are trying to decry at the time.

I'm sure that there will be some, staunchly eurosceptic, readers of this book who might well wish that there were no such thing as the European Union. In much the same way as the 'free lunch' comment, which seeks to highlight a generalised truth, I could easily say that there's no such thing as 'the European Union view' on anything.

The whole thing is deliberately, and incredibly, fragmented. In the United Kingdom we're used to having powerful governments elected under the First Past The Post system. The government of the day holds the power, and is held in check by Her Majesty's Official Opposition. That system served the UK reasonably well in a two-party era for much of the 20th century. The old Liberals had a clearly-defined geographical base, so that they still gained seats even when their national vote share was low.

There was an argument, even then, which could be made for proportional representation. When a constituency has elected the same party for 70 years without ever having a reasonable chance of going the other way, the minority in that constituency is - in effect

- permanently disenfranchised. There is nothing that their vote can ever realistically do to change anything, unless they move house to a more marginal constituency. They will always be represented by an MP whose views are opposed to their own. Their participation in democracy is often little more than an illusion. No wonder that people start to feel that politicians don't represent them, or that they can't make a difference!

The British system has many, many flaws. Its great advantage is that it produces **strong and stable leadership** in general. In recent times, it's failed to provide such leadership. There was the hung Parliament from 2010 to 2015, followed by a tiny Conservative majority from 2015 to 2017, before which Theresa May stood on a ticket of 'strong and stable' but was returned only as the largest party in a hung Parliament. This level of government instability is pretty much unprecedented in British history. It also masks considerable shifts in public opinion: to UKIP, and then away from UKIP, in England and Wales - and to the SNP in Scotland. There's a huge falling away in the Liberal Democrat vote since its high-water mark in 2010. It's not as if we've got inelastic elections producing the same indecisive result each time! We seem to have unstable instability, if you'll pardon the tautology. This is a new problem in the British system, and our system isn't set up very well to cope with it.

The other countries in the European Union, however, are generally much more used to the kind of bargaining and horse-trading that is associated with proportional representation. Instead of asking the question 'who has won the election?', they are much more likely to ask 'who can cobble together an alliance capable of taking more than half the votes in the Parliament?'. Parties are used to compromise, seeing their proposals watered down, or accepting that the price of getting one of their own proposals through must be supporting someone else's.

The European Parliament is like this, but more so. There are, at the time of writing, eight different political groups ranging from Left to Right (some would say far-Left to far-Right). Those who cannot fit into any of the eight groups are bundled together in the 'NI' group, which means non-inscrit, or in English, non-attached.

In Europe, unlike the UK, there *is* a clear and obvious far-right. The most extreme example of this is the Golden Dawn party, whose logo has something in common with a swastika - and whose roots were in those seeking to re-impose military dictatorship in Greece. Not even the BNP in the UK would have come close to being the kind of party that Golden Dawn is, especially given the history of violence associated with the latter.

This creates a strange kind of structure within the political groups: Marine Le Pen's Front National in France, seen by many as being far-right, refuses to allow parties such as Golden Dawn to be a part of their political group. Being too extreme for the Front National's tastes, Golden Dawn find themselves being non-inscrit.

The same thing happens on the far-left, though this is much less well-documented. Part of this has its roots in Eastern Europe, where many countries were under an oppressive Communist regime until a couple of decades ago. Ex-communists often found their way into mainstream left-leaning political parties. Those far-left groups tend to attract also the far-left populists who have started to spring up across the continent. In one case, an MEP now sitting with a far-left group had spent over a decade in prison for terrorist activity. Surprisingly, nobody seems to bat an eyelid about this in the European Parliament.

Within such a system, the so-called centre-left and centre-right political groups (though the phrase centre-right probably has a different meaning to that in the UK) generally work together with the Liberal group to push through the legislation that they want. It's common to see those groups working together as a single bloc. The compromise doesn't usually happen in the Parliament chamber, nor even in Committee, but through staffers frantically working together to find a back-door means by which a text can be agreed that both centre-left and centre-right are prepared to vote for.

In one sense, though, I've just fallen into the trap of seeing things in the British mindset. To understand what's going on at Westminster, first you need to understand what's going on in the elected House of Commons. Only then do other things (like the role of the unelected Lords - something which I believe is profoundly undemocratic in the UK and needs changing) actually matter. At the European Union level, the reverse is true. Unless you understand what's happening with the unelected European Commission, what's going on in the European Parliament makes little difference. That's because the Commission is the one to propose and drive forward legislation; the European Parliament is primarily a revising and amending chamber (although it can ask the Commission to legislate).

The European Commission, as a whole, is a much more political organisation than you would expect an unelected body to be. It is the Commission that holds a vision for what it wants the European Union to be. It is the Commission, generally, which rails against euroscepticism. It is the Commission, generally, which provides political leadership for the European Union. This is somewhat ironic, given that it describes itself on its own website as 'the EU's politically independent executive arm.' It is indeed politically independent in the sense that it can't be voted out by the people, but I suppose that they wouldn't want to put 'the EU's politically unaccountable executive arm' on their website! The Commission is hugely political, but it is not party-political. Commissioners do not represent their nations, but the European Union as a whole. Whilst Commissioners are chosen from each nation, their job is to forget national interests and consider only the European Union interest. For that reason, the Commission will often be the most hard-line when it comes to driving through harmonised EU legislation.

Meanwhile, the European Council consists of the heads of government of each member state of the European Union. Its job is more general; Prime Ministers and Presidents cannot together make detailed legislation in the way that the Commission can. They generally set overall priorities. They're elected and unelected at the same time: they may well be elected to their role as Prime Minister on an individual level, but their participation in the European Council is an ex-officio one. If you don't like what the European Council is doing, you can't vote it out at the next election to the European Council. You could, I suppose, vote for a different political party so that your representative in the European Council would be different, but that is never going to be the top issue at a domestic General Election. The public have a say in terms of electing the European Parliament. The public have no say in terms of electing the Commissioners. The public sort-of have a say in terms of choosing the European Council.

> The European Council is the one institution that has to be careful: if a PM works against their own national interests, they could run into trouble back home in the press.

How do all of these European institutions interact? Well, generally, when there's a difference of opinion, they repeat the process of 'bargaining and horse-trading' that I mentioned within the European Parliament - only at higher level.

They work to hammer out differences by convening a 'trialogue' (often written trilogue, but pronounced trialogue). This means that representatives of the Council, Parliament and Commission meet together to hammer out a compromise. The trilogue, in some ways, represents the main way that the European Union sorts out its direction.

So how does all of this affect Brexit?

Each of the three institutions has its own political priorities. These start to play out quite clearly when it comes to Brexit negotiations. Unlike when there are genuine differences at stake, each of these three institutions are actually easily able to accommodate the concerns of the other two because they don't actually contradict each other.

Normally, as with the European Union budget, these institutions all have genuine disagreements and have to compromise: national governments don't want to give the EU more money, whilst the Commission and Parliament do.

Here, though, it's different:

The European Commission...

- Is concerned about getting the best deal possible for the European Union
- Wants to centralise power at European Union level
- Seeks to prevent other members of the EU27 wanting to leave in the same way as the UK
- Wishes to ensure that the UK remains closely aligned to the European Union

The European Council...

- Wants to be seen to be defending their national interests back home
- Is nervous about the rise of euroscepticism in their own countries, and wants to show that Brexit doesn't work
- Seeks to find opportunities in Brexit to gain business from the United Kingdom, particularly in financial services
- Therefore, takes a hard line on questions including Northern

Ireland and Gibraltar

The European Parliament...

- Wants more power for the European Parliament, and for the European Union itself
- Is deeply aware that its only formal role in Brexit is to ratify any final Withdrawal Agreement
- Wishes to use Brexit as an opportunity to push for greater harmonisation and environmental standards
- Is deeply aware of elections coming up to the European Parliament in May 2019

If anyone wants to succeed in negotiations with the European Union, the key is to build a series of mini-alliances to make sure you've got enough votes to be able to do what you want.

When the United Kingdom voted to leave the European Union in June 2016, it didn't trigger Article 50 until the end of March 2017. What do you suppose that the European Union did during those 9 months? Do you suppose that it was sitting around, waiting for the United Kingdom to send it a letter stating that it was going to leave the European Union? Or was it spending the time making sure that it had its political priorities all mapped out?

The answer is simple. The UK spent those nine months on many things, but none of them really involved having a strategy for Brexit negotiations. We had a change of Prime Minister, including internal Conservative Party leadership election. We had the various court cases around Article 50, and then the Parliamentary legislation required to trigger it. Then, having triggered Article 50, the UK immediately held a General Election. Brexit was certainly an issue through all of this, but ***nobody in the UK was truly planning a negotiating strategy.*** The UK hadn't done enough in terms of civil service recruitment, and it didn't have a clear plan for how Brexit negotiations should go.

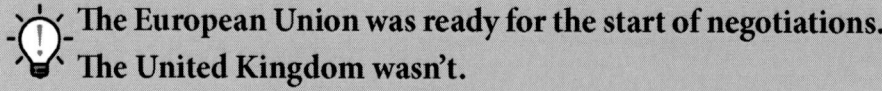

The European Union was ready for the start of negotiations. The United Kingdom wasn't.

The European Union was easily able to resolve the different things which the Commission, Council and Parliament all wanted: they could pretty much agree to act in such a way as to seek everything. There was no need for them to compromise on their own negotiating position, so they demanded the lot.

CHAPTER 10

NEGOTIATION: WHAT WENT WRONG FOR THE UK

"By failing to prepare, you are preparing to fail" - Benjamin Franklin

In the long nine months between the referendum and the triggering of Article 50, the European Union had been hard at work preparing for negotiations.

The EU27 had agreed to approach negotiations as a unified bloc. They knew what their negotiating positions were going to be, and determined that negotiation would not be seen in any way as an attempt between two equals.

After the Article 50 notification had been received, the European Council produced its guidelines for negotiation within a month. There was no way that the EU27 would have agreed something so detailed without preparation having taken place already. Those guidelines were a trap.

The guidelines sought to separate the negotiations into two distinct phases. The first would deal with financial arrangements, issues surrounding citizens' rights, and the bread-and-butter issues of withdrawal. The second would deal with the future relationship between the United Kingdom and the European Union. The European Council declared that "The European Council will monitor progress closely and determine when sufficient progress has been achieved to allow negotiations to proceed to the next phase". The phrase 'sufficient progress' was then to be determined solely by the European Union.

The United Kingdom was immediately turned into a supplicant: the question was always *'has the UK done enough to persuade the EU that sufficient progress has been made, so that negotiations can progress?'*

The UK did not have an alternative plan of its own, but the European Council's plan for structuring negotiations ensured almost from Day 1 that the UK would be unable to negotiate a good deal with the European Union.

Unfortunately, Theresa May had just called a General Election for June 8th - and the UK was considerably distracted. Whilst politicians were busy explaining to the public what they wanted from negotiations, nobody was asking the more important question: how to go about getting it.

In truth, this was the point at which everything went badly wrong for the UK. The UK was expected to agree on a number of things in Phase 1 of negotiations:

- How much money the UK would pay in a financial settlement (the 'divorce bill')
- The rights of EU citizens living in the UK, and UK citizens living in the EU
- The border between Northern Ireland and the Republic of Ireland

The UK also agreed, right from the beginning of negotiations, to continued co-operation in areas of research, security, defence and counter-terrorism.

Much of this doesn't seem particularly unreasonable at first glance, but let's pause for a moment. When the UK was negotiating with the European Union, what were the advantages and disadvantages which each side had?

European Union advantages

1. The European Union's market is substantially bigger than the UK's.

2. The EU27 is the world's *second-largest economy*. (Note: The Remain campaign claimed the EU to be the world's largest economy, which was only true if you also included the UK in those calculations)

3. The UK wishes to continue to export financial services to the European Union and to maintain the strength of the City of London

4. The changes caused by Brexit are larger for the UK than for the European Union. Therefore, it would take time for the UK economy to adapt.

United Kingdom advantages

1. There was no absolute legal requirement for the United Kingdom

to pay any kind of 'divorce bill' to the European Union. The European Union budget is incredibly difficult to agree. If the UK were to leave without paying into that budget, it would cause significant upheaval within the EU27.

2. The European Union would wish to continue working with the United Kingdom on areas where the United Kingdom is a global leader - namely research, security, defence, and counter-terrorism.

3. The UK is a significant net importer from the European Union. Consequently, in any no-deal scenario which resulted in a tariff-based regime, more tariff imports would be paid to the UK than to the European Union.

4. With (at the time) roughly 3.2 million EU citizens living in the UK, and 1.2 million UK citizens living in the EU, the scale of the issue regarding citizens was greater as far as the EU was concerned. Furthermore, a large proportion of UK citizens living in the EU were those who had retired there, and were bringing money from the UK to the European Union.

Which side had the stronger hand in negotiation? That's a matter of opinion. For example, on the economy, Brexiteers would say "*The UK is the EU's best customer. We buy far more from the EU than the EU buys from us*". Meanwhile, Remainers would say "*Yes, but that is still 44% of our exports and only 8% [or 18%] of the EU's total exports*". The figure should be 18% if you treat the EU as a single bloc, but 8% if you count internal EU trade (for example France selling goods to Germany) as being an export. Either way, Remainers argued, it's a higher percentage of our trade than it is of the EU's.

Brexiteers would then say "*Yes, but if you look at each pair of nations individually then in general the UK is in trade deficit with almost every other country*". Remainers would counter by saying that the UK is breaking that relationship with 27 countries all at once.

Which of the two is the bigger issue? Is Brexit in that case a bigger problem for the UK or for the EU27? It probably depends upon the country concerned, to some extent. A no-deal Brexit causes huge issues to the Republic of Ireland, but might be somewhat less noticeable to some other nations. Germany would struggle in specific industries (tariffs upon German car exports could be problematic) but the overall hit on its economy would be limited. The point can be argued either way. The European Union simply assumed that Brexit would cause more problems to the UK, and the UK never truly challenged that assertion.

In terms of trade, there were strong arguments to be made by both sides. The UK instantly threw away its other advantages. It started by guaranteeing rights for EU citizens living in the UK (making the bigger concession of the two), and then asking the European Union to do likewise for UK citizens living in the EU. The European Union did not immediately offer this guarantee.

It's certainly possible to make a moral case that the UK shouldn't use citizens' rights as a bargaining chip in negotiations. However, making a unilateral guarantee and then asking the European Union to do likewise was a clear mistake. It set the scene for future negotiations: the UK made an offer, and then made requests of the European Union.

The European Union's two-phase strategy placed the rest of the UK's negotiating cards firmly into the first phase of negotiations. The European Union operates on the principle that '*nothing is agreed until everything is agreed*'. In this case, they decided that the principle referred to each of the two phases of negotiation separately.

From the beginning, the UK's only reasonable option was to refuse to negotiate under those conditions. The European Union expected the UK to surrender every one of its trump cards, and agree to make substantial payments to the European Union, before even beginning to consider anything about the future trading relationship. From the UK's point of view, the two things had to be linked.

Instead, Theresa May took a different approach. She believed that by agreeing to calm all of the European Union's concerns on matters where the UK was a global leader, and making a unilateral agreement on citizens' rights, she would build up significant goodwill from the European Union.

That strategy was incredibly naive. The United Kingdom had systematically, one by one, given away everything that could reasonably have helped it to negotiate a good deal. The European Union made unrealistic demands (reportedly up to 100 billion euros) for the financial settlement, which bore no resemblance to reality. When the United Kingdom finally agreed on a figure around €39 billion, this was seen in the UK as a massive defeat for the United

Kingdom. In Brussels, there was no such consensus.

The United Kingdom was banking on being able to peel off some of the EU27, and using the typical approach of trying to build consensus with individual nations. This approach was never going to work: as in the previous chapter, the European Council, European Commission and European Parliament were all committed to working together as if a single unit. The European Parliament appointed Guy Verhofstadt as its chief Brexit negotiator. Recalling that under the Treaties, the European Parliament's only actual role in Brexit is to vote on the final deal, this was seen as a big 'win' for the European Parliament. That big win cost the Commission and Council nothing; Guy Verhofstadt is a euro-federalist who would be even more determined to strike a hard bargain with the UK.

At the Press Conference after the European Council summit, the Council President Donald Tusk said: "*I want to underline the outstanding unity of all the 27 leaders on the guidelines for our negotiations with the UK...we now have unanimous support from all the 27 member states and the EU institutions, giving us a strong political mandate for these negotiations.*"

The United Kingdom went along with the European Union's approach towards negotiations, completely failing to recognise the trap that it was falling into. The so-called 'divorce bill' is probably the best way to understand this.

As a member of the Budget Committee in the European Parliament, I was asked to give evidence to a House of Lords Select Committee about the divorce bill and the UK's commitments. The first question which I was asked was about the UK's legal obligations.

The European Union has a 7-year financial plan, known as the Multiannual Financial Framework. The current plan covers the years from 2014 to 2020, with the next plan being due for 2021 to 2027. Within that overall framework, each year the European Union has to agree its budget.

Clearly, in 2014, the United Kingdom agreed to participate in the Multiannual Financial Framework. My view, as I expressed to the Select Committee, was that this was a *moral obligation* and not a *legal obligation*. The difference between moral and legal obligations is clearly important when negotiating: irrespective of anything else, you have to pay any legal obligations. Moral obligations rest upon negotiation being undertaken in good faith: provided that the European Union is being reasonable with the United Kingdom, it reasonably follows that the United Kingdom should be reasonable with the European Union.

The amount of money involved here, from the United Kingdom continuing to participate in European Union programmes until the end of 2020, is something in the order of £20 billion. The question matters very much. My response to the Select Committee was along the following lines:

1. The MFF Regulation (which establishes the EU's 7-year financial plan) can be amended. Amendments envisaged within the regulations are as follows:

a) If a new country joins the EU, or

b) In unforeseen circumstances

2. The withdrawal of a member state is actually very, very rarely considered within the treaties. It is mentioned in Article 50 and in very few other places other than Article 50. It is rarely referred to in regulations or in other parts of European Union law. Clearly, when signing the MFF, Brexit was an unforeseen circumstance.

3. Why does the MFF Regulation say that it can be changed when a new country joins the EU? Presumably because accession of a new country changes the European Union's budgeting. A financial plan cannot realistically say the same when the number of countries in the EU has changed. It is, I argued, logically consistent to suppose that, with the withdrawal of a member state, the MFF may also be revised.

4. The nature of an 'unforeseen circumstance' is difficult to define. I mentioned the so-called 'elephant test' mentioned in British courts of law: you know it when you see it. Withdrawal from the European Union is something that has not happened, unless you consider Greenland. Something that has not happened at any time in the last 40 years is going to be an unforeseen circumstance, as far as the European Union is concerned.

5. Even if you were to argue that the MFF Regulation couldn't be amended, think of the status of a Regulation. Regulations are made under the Treaties. Article 50.3 of the Lisbon treaty states as follows:

"The treaties shall cease to apply to the state in question from the date of entry into force of the withdrawal agreement or, failing that, two years after the notification referred to in paragraph 2", and then it goes on to give the exception to that.

6. If, according to Article 50.3, the treaties no longer apply, then regulations made under the treaties should be considered to no longer apply, as a necessary consequence.

My argument, therefore, was that the UK had no legal obligation to pay this money.

I was challenged again by the Select Committee: I had referred very specifically to the *legal* position rather than the *moral* position. Why had I done so?

My response was simple: I argued that you can only make a concession if there is no legal obligation to do so, in order for it to be considered a concession in the first place. Otherwise it's merely following your obligations. I might well be prepared for the UK to make a concession, but it's important that concessions cut both ways. When we have a bargaining chip, we should not simply throw it away.

Assets and liabilities

The next problem with the EU divorce bill was about distribution of assets and liabilities. The European Union has more liabilities than it does assets; they argued that the UK needed to 'settle up' on its debts in the same way as you might settle a bar tab when leaving.

I'm not so sure that this is a fair analogy. If I resign my membership of a local golf club, I don't have to continue paying towards its mortgage.

Whilst the United Kingdom could ask the European Union for a share of its buildings, fine wine collection, and so on, it couldn't do so without equally having to accept liability for the monies owed by the European Union itself. These liabilities were described by the European Union as pensions and other employee benefits, borrowings, payables, accrued charges and deferred income, and what it describes as 'other liabilities'.

The European Union, at that time, had €226 billion in liabilities and just €154 billion in assets. The difference between the two was, broadly speaking, pension liabilities.

It could easily be argued that the UK should pay a share of pension liabilities. But what percentage would that be, even if the UK were to concede that? I argued to the Select Committee that:

Although the UK's gross contribution to the EU budget, after the rebate, is in the order of 12.5% of the total EU budget, the figure for British staff working in the European Union institutions is in the region of 4%. There are 3.8% in the Commission, 4.8% in the Parliament and 3.2% in the Council. Even if the European Union were to push that point, and even if, for whatever reason, that point were conceded, the question then would be whether we would concede that point at

12.5% of the EU's pension liability or at 4%. Personally, of course, I hope we do not reach the stage where we are conceding such points in negotiation.

4% of the outstanding pension commitments would have been something in the order of £2 to £2.5 billion.

So what does all this mean?

The UK did not have a legal responsibility to pay €39 billion (or so) to the European Union as a 'divorce bill'. The fact that the UK agreed to this was bad enough, but the bigger problem was that the UK agreed to it *without getting anything tangible in return.*

The UK had systematically given away every single advantage which it held in negotiation. Having done so, it proceeded to offer the European Union a huge financial settlement upon withdrawal. None of this was linked to the future trade relationship with the European Union in any way.

When the European Union finally decided to declare that 'sufficient progress' had been made to move to Phase 2 of negotiations, the United Kingdom was utterly powerless. From this point, negotiating a good deal was an impossibility for Theresa May.

The UK failed to challenge the EU's negotiating guidelines from Day 1; it wasn't prepared to walk away from the table. Everything else that went wrong followed on from that.

If all of this had been happening in a vacuum, it would have been bad enough. At the same time as the British government was woefully mishandling negotiations, opposition politicians were actively encouraging the European Union not to offer the United Kingdom a better deal.

In a Channel 4 series, Carry On Brexit, a meeting was shown between Guy Verhofstadt (the European Parliament's Brexit negotiator), Professor AC Grayling, and Catherine Bearder - a Liberal Democrat MEP. Remain campaigner Professor Grayling said "What would help the remain movement in the UK...if the EU is very tough and uncompromising on a deal". Catherine Bearder added "I'm absolutely convinced that within a decade we'll be knocking on the door".

Whilst Professor Grayling's words - actually asking the European Union not to concede anything to the UK - are more direct than most, other opposition UK politicians consistently poured scorn upon the very notion that the UK could get a good deal from the EU. They essentially took the European Union line throughout negotiations, which could not possibly have done anything other than to make it harder for Theresa May to negotiate.

In October 2017, the European Parliament voted on a resolution about its own view on Brexit negotiations. On behalf of the EFDD Group in the European Parliament, I tabled a number of amendments to the Parliament's position. Each of my thirteen amendments were rejected. What should have been surprising, though, was the number of British MEPs who voted against such amendments as:

Insists that the EU must not obstruct or delay any negotiations by the UK Government that seek trade agreements with third countries, provided that such agreements are intended to commence on a date after the end of March 2019

This amendment goes back to the meaning of the phrase 'sincere co-operation' which I mentioned at the end of Chapter 5. British MEPs were, literally, voting against the principle that their own government shouldn't be allowed to start working on free trade agreements with third countries. Without doing such a thing, how could they possibly expect to be able to show the European Union that the UK was serious about being prepared for Brexit?

I sought to amend a one-sided piece of text about citizens' rights to make sure that citzens' rights should be seen as equally important in both directions: UK citizens living in the EU should be treated just as well as EU citizens living in the UK. Another piece suggested that the United Kingdom should still be subject to European Court of Justice rulings regarding citizens post-Brexit. I tried to change it to something far more equitable:

Believes that there can and should be a swift resolution regarding reciprocal rights of residence in respect of EU citizens in the UK and UK citizens in the EU-27; stresses that after the UK formally leaves the EU such rights should be adjudicated by the judicial authorities of the relevant jurisdiction in accordance with the exclusive exercise of the sovereign rights of that jurisdiction and without subordination to those of a third party;

Each time, I could only watch in horror as other British MEPs consistently voted against. The Conservatives were, to be fair to them, split - but Labour, Liberal Democrats, SNP and Greens generally voted against every attempt to ensure fairness.

Other amendments designed to ensure that Gibraltar should be treated fairly, and that the European Court of Justice should not have jurisdiction in the UK post-Brexit, met with similar fates.

Strangely, one British Labour MEP did vote in favour of my amendment suggesting that the European Union should publish its no-deal assessments. I've often wondered why: was it a simple mistake, as can often happen in the European Parliament, or did he realise that when British politicians demanded that the UK government should produce their assessments of no-deal Brexit, that the Commission should do the same?

I suspect (but am not 100% sure) that it was a simple mistake; if an influential Labour MEP were intentionally voting that way, then others might well have followed. Mistakes can happen. In one day alone in December 2018, the European Parliament voted over 800 times. You have to concentrate just to keep track of every vote, let alone attempt to understand the full ramifications of everything.

I return to my earlier question. When opposition politicians kept banging the drum for the European Union, telling the media and everyone else in the UK that a good deal was impossible, how were we possibly supposed to expect the European Union to compromise? When politicians continued fighting the referendum campaign after the referendum was over, nobody on the EU side would truly want to bargain with the UK if they thought that their aims could be furthered by refusing to back down.

The EU refused to back down. I'm not sure whether to blame the British government more, or the opposition. Both were culpable; both led us to Theresa May's eventual deal.

All of this brings us to the current fork in the road. In the next chapters I'll take a look at the various possibilities that have been suggested for what happens next:

- What would happen if the UK decided not to leave after all?
- Is the Norway option viable?
- Could we negotiate a Canada-style free trade deal with the EU?
- What does Theresa May's deal actually do?
- The No-Deal scenario
- Does the 'second referendum' make sense?

CHAPTER 11

WHAT WOULD REMAIN ACTUALLY MEAN?

Over a number of years, some anti-EU campaigners have consistently held the view that 'it's now or never' when it comes to leaving the European Union. Before the Nice Treaty, the claim was made that it could leave us virtually powerless to leave. The same was said about the Lisbon Treaty. Each time there is a deadline: we were told, for example, that if the UK did not trigger Article 50 by April 2017, we would be unable to do so without the consent of other EU nations.

The reason was supposedly to do with changes to the system of calculating majorities under Qualified Majority Voting (QMV) in the European Union. The changes were actually taking place, but they didn't impact upon Article 50. They merely impacted upon the other nations' reactions to Brexit. I lost count of the number of times I received panicked emails from constituents and others, concerned that the UK would lose the power to leave if we didn't trigger Article 50 by the end of March.

The whole thing just wasn't true: nothing in the Lisbon Treaty prevents a Member State from deciding to leave the European Union in accordance with its own constitutional requirements. Indeed, that's precisely what the Lisbon Treaty itself says! In purely legal terms, Remaining in the European Union wouldn't prevent us from leaving in the future. The European Courts would not allow the UK to reverse the Article 50 negotiation as a delaying tactic - for example, we couldn't reverse it and then immediately re-trigger it to re-set the clock for another two years. However, the 'remedy' then would be to say that the revocation would have been void rather than the notification itself! This, for those in favour of Brexit, might not be a bad thing.

Supposing that, for whatever reason, British politicians found a means of overturning Brexit. In that case, the issue would not go away. It seems almost certain that in such circumstances, a new political party would be formed to fight for Brexit. The social consequences, as I suggested in an earlier chapter, would be profound. In this chapter, we're going to take a quick look at the direction in which the European Union is heading. The European Union in five years' time will not be the same as the European Union of early 2019. I'm not going to deal with 'maybes' in this chapter. It's unlikely now that Turkey will join the European Union, and it's equally unlikely that the UK will be forced to adopt the euro. The European Union is, however, seeking to expand its influence in various ways:

Remain means changes to taxation at EU level...

The European Union has, since 2014, been pushing strongly for taxation to be more centralised and harmonised at EU level. Why? Not just because it wants a higher budget for itself, but because it doesn't like the current political situation. At present, the EU has to negotiate its annual budget with Member States in the Council which don't want to increase contributions. The more money the EU can collect directly, the less need for such negotiations. If it needs more money, it can then simply amend the rate of whichever tax it is looking at.

The European Union budget in each year from 2014-2020 is limited by the European Union's seven-year financial plan known as the Multiannual Financial Framework (MFF). This places an upper bound on the size of the European Union budget each year, above which funds can only be raised in specific circumstances. If the UK were still contributing to the European Union budget, there would be huge political will to negotiate higher boundaries for the following MFF. This would lead to greater UK contributions than projected. Broadly speaking, ***Remain means that the cost of EU membership will increase.*** I anticipate that this increase would be substantial in 2021, with a huge jump in 2028.

The Financial Transaction Tax and the Common Consolidated Corporate Tax Base

The European Commission claimed in early 2017 that proposals for an EU-wide Financial Transaction Tax would be ready by mid-2017. Due to various political considerations including the Brexit negotiations, it appears that this will take slightly longer than the EU had originally planned. However, the political will from the Commission is clear. It is almost inconceivable that, if the UK were either in the European Union or subject to its legislation, the Financial Transaction Tax would not be in place within the next 5-10 years (and probably sooner). A Financial Transaction Tax would impact the United Kingdom disproportionately due to the prominence of the City of London. It is not clear that the UK would retain any power of veto, nor whether (in particular if a Labour government were in power at the time) if would use it if it could.

The effect upon the UK's financial services industry - which is far more reliant upon that industry than the rest of the European Union - would be significant, and deleterious.

The European Parliament has also regularly voted in facour of the Common Consolidated Corporate Tax Base. This would begin by having a single set of rules to calculate companies' taxable profits in the EU. When trading cross-border, there would be a certain usefulness for business in having to only obey one set of rules. The negative part? That it centralises control over business policy at European Union level, risking the United Kingdom losing its competitive advantage. Having agreed a common means of calculating profit and taxing that profit, it is only a short step to the European Union taking a percentage of it in direct taxation - or setting rules for which rates can be applied.

Environmental legislation and targets

The European Union's approach to environmental legislation is heavily target-orientated. This leads to substantial inefficiencies; it is clear from the direction of travel that the inefficiencies caused by EU energy policy are likely to persist - which will exacerbate energy price issues within the UK, having an impact on domestic customers as well as creating a potential loss of business and jobs. The European Union is constantly pushing further such targets. The first (and most major) problem with its approach is that it leads to the outsourcing of pollution. When the European Union artificially inflates energy prices in the UK and other Member States, the consequence is that the entire EU becomes less competitive globally. When that happens, energy-intensive industries close down in Europe and are replaced by others in countries with lower environmental standards, often India and China. This hurts economies in Europe, and also leads to lower environmental standards.

The second problem with the European Union's approach is that the nature of subsidies is distorting. A while ago, I came across an example relating to biomass after visiting a factory in my constituency which makes wood panelling products.

When a tree in the UK is cut down, it needs to be dried out (up to 50% of the weight is likely to be water due to our wet climate) and then processed. Pretty much every part of the tree is useful for something. Even sawdust can be used for example in the production of chipboard.

Whatever the wood itself has been used for, at the end of its life it can be recycled. Once the nails and other contaminants have been removed, it can be used again. At each stage of the process, there will be some dust which isn't really suitable for making anything. It might be that, on average, the same piece of wood could be used and recycled six times. In that time, it has perhaps been an internal door, a kitchen surface, laminate flooring and a chest of drawers.

Before government subsidies were available, they found a use for the leftover dust: they built their own biomass plant which is used to power and heat the factory. They have efficiency rates of over 90%. This kind of process is efficient and environmentally-friendly, business-driven and highly successful.

When the UK, as a result of EU renewables targets, introduced subsidies into that marketplace, the entire system changed.

> 💡 **When the government subsidises anything, you end up with more of it. Subsidising inefficiency is a bad idea.**

Subsidies led to many more companies wanting to build their own biomass plants, but without the same joined-up thinking. Other biomass plants set up, which chopped down trees and used them as a source of fuel. With no drying, no recycling and no co-ordination, their efficiency rates were far lower. Some plants were using the biomass only as a source of power, losing the heat altogether.

These biomass plants then created a demand for more wood, which can't immediately be supplied because it takes perhaps 30-40 years for a new tree to grow to maturity. The supply/demand equation having changed, the price of wood increased.

There are far more sensible means by which we could improve the quality of our environment, but the approach taken by the United Kingdom as members of the European Union is fundamentally flawed. A completely different approach is clearly needed. The European Union is continuing to double down on its current attitude towards the environment and climate change.

There is a significant correlation between anti-EU sentiment and belief that human beings are not responsible for causing climate change. The two need not go together: it is entirely possible for someone to accept the scientific consensus around climate change, yet also believe that the European Union is approaching the problem in a way that is fundamentally flawed.

One of the big mistakes often made by Leave campaigners was to try to convince people that climate change is not caused by human beings. It is a bad approach: convincing someone of one new idea (that Brexit is a good thing) is difficult enough in a single conversation; trying to convince them of a second (that climate change is not caused by human beings) makes the chances of success even more remote.

What Leave campaigners should have done, in such situations, is to instead point out the inefficiencies caused by the European Union's approach.

A European Army?

Angela Merkel, the Chancellor of Germany, was absolutely clear in November 2018 that she sought the creation of a European Army. This was broadly in accordance with the words of Commission President Jean-Claude Juncker. It is clear from Angela Merkel's words that a European Army is very much part of the thinking of the European Union:

The times when we could rely on others are over. This means nothing less than for us Europeans to take our destiny in our own hands if we want to survive as a Union. This means, in the long run, Europe has to become more capable to act. We have to reconsider our ways of deciding and to renounce the principle of unanimity where the European treaties allow and wherever this is necessary. I proposed a European security council, in which important decisions can be prepared faster. We have to create a European intervention unit with which Europe can act on the ground where necessary. We have taken major steps in the field of military cooperation, this is good and largely supported in this house. But I also have to say, seeing the developments of the recent years, that we have to work on a vision to establish a real European army one day.

French President Emanuel Macron has also called for a 'real European Army'. His words - and I'm giving them in French as well as English for a reason - were as follows:

nous devons nous protéger, a l'égard de la Chine, de la Russie, même des Etats-Unis.

This was translated in various ways - suggesting that he said the European Union needs to 'protect ourselves', or alternatively, 'defend ourselves', from China, Russia, and even/the same as the USA. Now, to be absolutely fair to President Macron, he wasn't suggesting a European Army to defend against American military aggression, as some newspapers translated it. He clarified in the speech by saying "we need a Europe that is increasingly able to defend itself by itself – and without solely depending on the USA".

Indeed, by November 2018, they were even arguing about who should have credit for the principle of a European Army. A Commission spokesman said:

Let me clarify that the first one who spoke about the EU Army four years ago was someone called Jean-Claude Juncker. Memory is short nowadays in Brussels and the capitals but people here present, you are aware of who launched this idea. We are delighted that both the president of the French Republic and the German Chancellor, with a few days interval, publicly backed this idea. We have many times explained how we see these things: this is a Commission that wants Europe to have a meaningful defence identity.

The European Army is not yet a reality, but European policy is already heading in that direction. The European Union has had a European Defence Agency since 2004. It is continuing to develop its Common Security and Defence Policy, which it describes as follows:

The Common Security and Defence Policy (CSDP) enables the Union to take a leading role in peace-keeping operations, conflict prevention and in the strengthening of the international security. It is an integral part of the EU's comprehensive approach towards crisis management, drawing on civilian and military assets.

It is clear that the European Union is keen on heading in a direction towards a European Army, though whether that ends up being a fully-fledged military remains to be seen. Either way, it is likely to prove problematic for many in the United Kingdom: the UK has a tradition of staunch support for NATO.

CHAPTER 12

THE NORWAY OPTION

If a politician wants to pay lip-service to the idea of leaving the European Union without getting any of the actual benefits, seeking a Norway-style arrangement between the United Kingdom and the European Union may well be the option for them.

Before the referendum, pro-European Union politicians were keen on pointing out the flaws in the Norwegian relationship with the European Union. As former Prime Minister Gordon Brown wrote in the Guardian, "even Norwegians oppose the Norwegian option". He wasn't wrong, at least not on that part. The rest of the article poured scorn upon everyone, and everything, that was anti-European Union, in the usual style of the time. David Cameron famously referred to Norway's relationship with the EU as being 'fax democracy'.

Norway is a member of the European Economic Area (EEA) and the European Free Trade Area (EFTA), but not a member of the European Union itself. It therefore has to obey the rules of the Single Market, including what europhiles describe as 'free movement of people' and eurosceptics describe as 'unlimited immigration'. Not only that, it is also a member of the Schengen Area so it has even less control over its borders than the UK has, whilst in the European Union. As a member of the Single Market, Norway must obey all EU regulations that relate to the Single Market. Furthermore, Norway has to pay into the EU budget for the privilege of having that access to the Single Market. The phrase 'fax democracy' suggests that Norway has little or no say in the new laws affecting the Single Market, so it simply has to sit and wait for the European Union to tell it what its new laws are going to be. This would be a bad option for the United Kingdom, but upon closer examination it is not necessarily quite so bad as it is often made out by eurosceptics.

The Norway option is, in my view, preferable to remaining in the European Union. It's still a long way from ideal.

1. Norway only has to obey some European Union legislation

Norway does have to obey all the EU legislation that relates to the Single Market, but that's all. When the European Union legislates on any other matter, Norway does not have to obey those laws.

2. It's not totally true to say that Norway has no say in EU laws

Norway, compared with the size of its population, actually has more say than the United Kingdom does in some areas. Many Single Market regulations now enforce standards and agreements from other international organisations. Suppose, for example, that there is an agreement made at the International Labour Organisation which is then translated into European Union law. In this case, Norway is effectively consulted twice before the UK is consulted at all:

a) Norway has a say at the ILO
b) The European Commission is required to consult Norway initially when putting forward new legislation

It's perfectly fair to say that Norway doesn't have a formal vote at EU level to attempt to prevent the European Union legislation, but what say would it actually have if it did? It would likely have 10-14 MEPs out of 750 in the European Parliament; it's vanishingly unlikely that less than 2% of the votes would actually make a difference. It would fare a little better in the Council under Qualified Majority Voting, but not much better.

Does Norway actually do better, through being consulted twice, than having a vote at a later stage when it would struggle to block anything? It's arguable that perhaps it does.

Norway also has what is known as a 'right of reservation' meaning that it can, in certain circumstances, refuse to follow a new EU law which goes against Norwegian interests. That right is limited in scope, at least in practice. For example, in 2011 Norway refused to implement the Postal Services Directive. The Postal Services Directive caused huge problems to the UK because of the way that some Royal Mail services had to be opened up to competition. Indeed, many eurosceptics blame the Postal Services Directive for the closure of Post Offices across the United Kingdom.

The problem? Norway came under a lot of pressure after refusing to implement the Postal Services Directive. Two years later, in 2013, it eventually gave in.

If the UK had a similar arrangement with the European Union, it's likely that the UK - a market of 60+ million people - would have a better chance at holding out than Norway, a market of just over 5 million people.

3. Yes, Norway does have to pay into the EU budget - but would the UK?

Norway is a substantial net exporter to the European Union. As such, its negotiating position is weak: it wants European Union countries to accept its goods without the imposition of tariffs. Under any standard tariff-based regime, Norway would lose out.

In plain terms (and I'm over-simplifying here), if Norway weren't in the EEA, Norway would have to pay the EU more in tariffs than the EU would have to be Norway.

The oversimplification lies, of course, in the fact that tariffs are paid by businesses rather than by nations - and it can be argued both ways in that context: tariffs distort competition, but they also impact upon the price paid by the consumer. Still, the Norwegian bargaining position is incredibly weak compared with the European Union's. It needs to be able to sell into European markets.

The UK's position would be different: it is a substantial net importer from the European Union. Under a Norway-style agremeent with the European Union, the UK would have a much stronger case.

4. The UK isn't already a part of the Schengen Area

Under a Norway-style arrangement with the European Union, it is unlikely that the UK would be required to join the Schengen Area. Norway chose to; the UK would not.

5. The European Economic Area provides for an 'emergency brake' to control immigration, which EU membership does not

Article 112 of the Agreement on the European Economic Area permits either Norway or the European Union to take safeguarding measures:

1. If serious economic, societal or environmental difficulties of a sectorial or regional nature liable to persist are arising, a Contracting Party may unilaterally take appropriate measures under the conditions and procedures laid down in Article 113.

2. Such safeguard measures shall be restricted with regard to their scope and duration to what is strictly necessary in order to remedy the situation. Priority shall be given to such measures as will least disturb the functioning of this Agreement.

3. The safeguard measures shall apply with regard to all Contracting Parties.

Article 113 then goes on to detail how this emergency brake may be applied. In the event that uncontrolled immigration is causing a specific problem, there is a time-limited option to take action to deal with that problem.

Whilst this wouldn't give the UK full control back over its

immigration system by any means, it still provides more flexibility than European Union membership.

6. Norway is outside the Common Agricultural Policy and Common Fisheries Policy

The Common Fisheries Policy, in particular, has been unpopular in the United Kingdom for a number of years. The thought that the UK could have the opportunity to regain control over fisheries under a Norway-style agreement would be immensely attractive to many people in the United Kingdom. However, the European Union would likely be hugely resistant to the UK regaining control over this area and would doubtless seek in negotiations to prevent that happening: many jobs of EU workers would be at risk.

Conclusion

One of the fundamental reasons for the Leave vote was a desire to give the United Kingdom the option to negotiate its own free trade deals worldwide. Under the Norway option, this would in effect be impossible.

The Norway option is clearly a bad option for the UK. Neither is it entirely clear that the Norway option is in fact available to the United Kingdom: as the leader of Norway's European Movement, Heidi Nordby Lunde, has said:

Really, the Norwegian option is not an option. We have been telling you this for one and a half years since the referendum and how this works, so I am surprised that after all these years it is still part of the grown-up debate in the UK. You just expect us to give you an invitation rather than consider whether Norway would want to give you such an invitation. It might be in your interest to use our agreement, but it would not be in our interest.

This view is not universally shared in Norway; the Norwegian Prime Minister Erna Solberg has been more accommodating, saying that Norway would 'examine' the possibility of the UK being a part of the European Economic Area.

It's also not entirely clear that Norway would have the power to reject the UK being in the European Economic Area, even if it wanted to: the UK's membership of the European Economic Area is not clearly derived from its membership of the European Union: the Agreement establishing the European Economic Area being separate from the Treaties on the European Union, it's at least arguable that the UK can simply choose to leave the EU without leaving the EEA should it so wish.

The bigger question, though, is whether the United Kingcom would want such an arrangement with the European Union in the first place. Norwegian politicians describe it as asking whether the United Kingdom would want to go from 'rule maker to rule taker'.

Having said all of that, the Norway option may be a bad option - but it is not the worst option on the table. Norwegian politicians have been scathing about Norway's deal with the European Union, but Norwegian voters have twice rejected joining the European Union in referenda in 1972 and 1994. Opinion polls today show that, if the public were asked, a wider majority would vote to reject EU membership. However bad Norway's deal is, the people of Norway do seem to prefer that deal to actual membership of the European Union. If the only three available options were the Norway option, remaining in the European Union, and Theresa May's Withdrawal Agreement, it's certainly possible that the Norway option would be the least-bad of the three. Still, that doesn't make it in any way a good deal.

One reasonable possibility for the UK would be to use the Norway option as a temporary holding position whilst negotiating something else, possibly a Canada-style deal. This isn't as far-fetched as it sounds, because of the lack of a Parliamentary majority for other options - and the likelihood for the UK Parliament being absolutely determined to avoid a no-deal Brexit under any circumstances.

CHAPTER 13

THE CANADA OPTION

I've never fully understood why Canada, or the various alternatives described as Canada-plus, Canada-plus-plus, or even Canada-plus-plus-plus, haven't been the default option for the United Kingdom right from the start of negotiations. This may be somewhat more complicated now, given the timescales involved with Brexit.

Broadly speaking, the reasons for voting for Brexit were as follows:

- Regaining the ability for the UK to negotiate trade deals
- Regaining control over immigration
- Ending the jurisdiction of European courts in the UK
- Regaining control of fisheries and farming
- Bringing sovereignty back to the UK
- Avoiding paying the annual membership fee to the EU
- Stopping EU regulations from affecting businesses that don't trade with the European Union

There are others, but most of the common reasons are as described above. Some might mention a desire to leave the European Court of Human Rights as a reason for supporting Brexit, but this is a little more complicated than it seems: the Court of Human Rights isn't actually an EU court. However, if a country is a member of the EU then it is also obliged to be a member of the European Court of Human Rights.

Other people might mention concerns over the rule of law, such as the means by which the European Arrest Warrant is used. Various minor arguments in terms of animal welfare have been put forward, and there are any number of other questions raised when it comes to the nature of how democratic the European Union is. Eurosceptics generally consider the EU to be undemocratic and unreformable; europhiles tend to either believe that it is already democratic, or that it can be reformed to become democratic.

I don't, however, think that any of these arguments were main drivers for the Brexit vote - except to the extent that questions about how democratic the European Union is impacts upon the question of sovereignty (the old 'who governs Britain?' question as posed by UKIP in 2004).

The seven reasons in the bullet-points on the previous page are probably the best way to test any potential Brexit deal: if it does all seven of those, then it's very difficult for even the most ardent eurosceptic to argue that the referendum hasn't been respected.

In this chapter, I'm not going to distinguish particularly between the different Canada models. That's a little too technical to go into in this book, and the exact levels of co-operation beyond a free trade deal would necessarily depend on negotiation. For the rest of the chapter, I'm going to assume that we're looking at a model which incorporates a wide-ranging free trade deal and permits the obvious bilateral means of co-operation in areas such as security and intelligence where it would make sense for the United Kingdom and the European Union to work together as neighbours. Straightforward matters such as mutual recognition of qualifications, or a short-term visa waiver scheme to allow tourists to travel freely to and from the United Kingdom, would be reasonable assumptions as part of such a deal.

The idea of striking an ambitious free trade deal between the United Kingdom and the European Union along the lines of the EU-Canada trade deal is one which pretty much passes all seven of these tests. Another way of looking at it is this: it is the closest possible relationship which we could have with the European Union as our neighbours without losing any of the major drivers of the Brexit vote. In short, a properly-negotiated Canada-style deal would leave nobody saying 'Brexit has been betrayed' but would leave the UK and the EU as close neighbours, partners and allies.

EU Council President Donald Tusk, in March 2018, joined the President of the European Parliament, Antonio Tajani, in suggesting that such an option could work for the United Kingdom. (The European Union has five Presidents - apologies if it's a little difficult at times to keep up!)

Tajani suggested that a UK-EU trade deal could be deeper than the EU-Canada one. Donald Tusk was, perhaps, speaking out of a little frustration. He seemed dismissive, suggesting that this approach was what remained when closer co-operation had to be ruled out, thanks to the UK's red lines. For many back in the UK, it was precisely what they wanted to hear:

Therefore, it should come as no surprise that the only remaining

possible model is a free trade agreement. I hope that it will be ambitious and advanced – and we will do our best, as we did with other partners, such as Canada recently – but anyway it will only be a trade agreement.

I propose that we aim for a trade agreement covering all sectors and with zero tariffs on goods. Like other free trade agreements, it should address services. And in fisheries, reciprocal access to fishing waters and resources should be maintained.

Up to this point, it all seems like pretty much plain sailing. That doesn't mean that there aren't a couple of problems with it, however. Note the language relating to fishing rights, for example. The European Union retaining access to British fishing waters is one thing; however, the continuation of the current situation where EU boats fish far more of the value of fish in British waters than UK boats do? That would be quite another.

Broadly speaking, though, it seemed that Tusk was saying what many British eurosceptics wanted to hear. There would be two obvious bones of contention, were this option to be explored. Firstly, the Irish border question needed to be resolved. In this sense, the EU 'divide and conquer' strategy as far as Northern Ireland was concerned would be critical. Tusk made it quite clear that the offer would not include Northern Ireland in the situation that the border question had not been resolved. Given the smoke-and-mirror tactics being employed over that border issue, this would have proved to be a major challenge.

The second problem would be financial services. Whilst Tusk's words suggested that the agreement should 'address services', it isn't totally clear precisely what is meant by this.

Services really do matter to any UK trade relationship with other countries. Again oversimplifying, the UK generally imports goods and exports services. The UK is the world's second-largest exporter of services, of which a huge proportion is financial services.

In any trade deal that the UK wished to strike with a third country, we'd basically be saying this: *We'll import your stuff without slapping tariffs on them, so long as you allow your customers to buy services from us without regulating us out of the market.* A free trade deal that's only about goods doesn't help us to sell things; a free trade deal that's only about services wouldn't work well for other countries. To work for both parties, any trade deal that we strike pretty much anywhere in the world should include a quid-pro-quo.

This is where the whole thing starts to get a little bit tricky. Goods and services have become packaged together in recent years. Buying an iPhone? What is it that you're buying - is it the physical product, or is it the software that's installed on it? How do you deal with something that's both a good and a service at the same time? What about a product that's sold with insurance or with regular online updates to the product over a period of time?

When you start to think about it in the context of a modern technology-driven world, goods and services just can't be separated out in quite the same way that they used to be.

Tusk's words mention 'services', but critically they don't mention 'financial services'. Whether negotiating a Canada-style deal would lead to a good deal for the United Kingdom would depend very much upon what the arrangements might be for financial services. So whilst it seemed that some at European Union level were quite encouraging, the French Economy Minister Bruno Le Maire said:

Financial services aren't goods. They cannot be traded and supervised in the same way. Once a country decides to leave there are consequences: you simply can't be 'in' and 'out' at the same time.

These words, like much in politics, seem to be both true and untrue at the same time. At face value, it makes sense. But it's a very protectionist view of the European Union's markets. When the UK sells financial services to other countries, we don't need to be part of a political union to do so. Provided that UK companies obey EU legislation when selling financial services to customers in the European Union, there doesn't need to be a problem. The question, though, is the direction in which the EU itself is headed.

The UK does more clearing of euro-denominated contracts than the eurozone does. Much of the UK's work relies upon relatively low regulation and taxation of the kinds of trades which are essential to the functioning of global financial markets. Meanwhile, the European Union seems to be heading in a very different direction. It's pushing the Financial Transaction Tax model, which would make businesses within the European Union vastly uncompetitive once that goes ahead. Consequently, the European Union sees an opportunity in Brexit: to try to limit the amount of financial services business that the UK is able to do in EU countries, so that the EU is able to protect its own business once the EU becomes more uncompetitive.

The Canada-style approach isn't necessarily an absolute, nailed-on, guaranteed solution to all of the UK's problems. To ensure a good deal along those lines would require months of painstaking negotiations over the Irish border and financial services at the very least. Nevertheless, there are huge advantages to both sides of such an approach.

As late as October 2018, Donald Tusk was still saying the same kind of thing:

From the very beginning, the EU offer has been not just a Canada deal, but a Canada-plus-plus-plus deal. Much further-reaching on trade, on internal security and on foreign policy cooperation. This is a true measure of respect and this offer remains in place. The EU is serious about getting the best possible deal. Even though we haven't changed our minds that the consequences of Brexit will be negative, for both sides.

Once again, leading Brexiteers urged Theresa May to take Donald Tusk at his word.

In the meantime, time has ticked by for a further three months. With Brexit Day looming, it seems that the window of opportunity for such a deal is slipping. Yet a Canada-style deal is the only type of deal which could reasonably be expected to lead to a future trading relationship which truly respects the result of the referendum.

The difficulty now with the Canada option isn't whether it's right for the UK or not. The difficulty is whether, given that Theresa May has pushed her own deal for a lengthy period of time, there is any realistic prospect of making it happen.

The Canada option is very much worth exploring, but with time running out, there isn't a clear and obvious way for it to be properly explored before the deadline.

CHAPTER 14

THE THERESA MAY DEAL

There's an old saying that a camel is what a horse would look like if it had been designed by a committee. Theresa May's Withdrawal Agreement is a bit like that: it is wrapped up in convoluted wording designed to confuse.

The Agreement is in two parts: the 585-page legally binding Withdrawal Agreement, and the 26-page Political Declaration. The Withdrawal Agreeement describes the process of the transition period and the legal basis upon which everything should happen from March 29th 2019 onwards until the end of the transition period. The Political Declaration is much more vague, describing the terms of the enduring future relationship between the United Kingdom and the European Union.

When reading through the 585-page Withdrawal Agreement, there is a very strong sense that it's not designed to be readable to the average person. If the average person were to read through it, line by line, like I've done, they still wouldn't be much closer to understanding what the significance of the document actually is.

To give one example, Article 34 of the draft Withdrawal Agreement refers to administrative co-operation between the United Kingdom and the European Union:

1. By way of derogation from Articles 7 and 128(1), as of the date of entry into force of this Agreement, the United Kingdom shall have the status of observer in the Administrative Commission. It may, where the items on the agenda relating to this Title concern the United Kingdom, send a representative, to be present in an advisory capacity, to the meetings of the Administrative Commission and to the meetings of the bodies referred to in Articles 73 and 74 of Regulation (EC) No 883/2004 where such items are discussed.

2. By way of derogation from Article 8, the United Kingdom shall take part in the Electronic Exchange of Social Security Information (EESSI) and bear the related costs.

This is typical of the Withdrawal Agreement as a whole. The Agreement regularly refers to European Union legislation, linking to the legislation rather than setting out the actual meaning within the wording. Article 34 isn't anything particularly pernicious in and of itself, but unless you read it in conjunction with Regulation 883/2004 then it doesn't make that much sense. As it happens, this is related to data processing. The United Kingdom will continue to pay the 'related costs' for the Electronic Exchange of Social Security Information. How much money is the UK expected to pay towards this? What is the UK's share in this context? These costs aren't spelled out in the Withdrawal Agreement, nor in the relevant EU legislation.

The whole of Article 34 is written in such a way as to be unintelligible to the average person. Even the average politician, expected to vote on the Draft Withdrawal Agreement, is unlikely to be able to understand all of the intricacies of what is written here. The people supposed to vote on the final deal will not, in general, truly know what they're actually voting on. Jeremy Corbyn famously admitted to not even having read the Withdrawal Agreement.

How did I choose Article 34 specifically? I did it at random, scrolling part of the way through the document and choosing the first Article that I happened to see. I didn't choose a particularly over-the-top example. In fact, I probably chose one of the less critical parts.

Each reference to European Union legislation requires an understanding of the relevant EU legislation.

But who are the interpreters of what is meant by European Union legislation? The European Courts! When Theresa May claims that the UK will not be bound specifically by the decisions of the European Union's courts under this Agreement, that may technically be true - but in practice, the meaning of European Union legislation is interpreted and defined by the European Union's courts.

When Theresa May gave her Mansion House speech at the start of March 2018, eurosceptics generally cheered her comment that

In the future, the EU treaties and hence EU law will no longer apply in the UK. The agreement we reach must therefore respect the sovereignty of both the UK and the EU's legal orders. That means the jurisdiction of the ECJ in the UK must end. It also means that the ultimate arbiter of disputes about our future partnership cannot be the court of either party.

In fact, eurosceptics were so pleased by those words that they generally glossed over - or missed - the other words in that same speech on the subject of European Union courts:

When we leave the EU, the Withdrawal Bill will bring EU law into UK law. That means cases will be determined in our courts. But, where appropriate, our courts will continue to look at the ECJ's judgments, as they do for the appropriate jurisprudence of other countries' courts.

And if, as part of our future partnership, Parliament passes an identical law to an EU law, it may make sense for our courts to look at the appropriate ECJ judgments so that we both interpret those laws consistently.

When those are words referring to the UK acting of its own volition, they might draw a sharp intake of breath from some people. I can imagine some people asking questions like '*Why should the United Kingdom consult the European Union on its own law?*' or similar. But so long as it's clearly voluntary, there's no specific harm done. The difference, though, is twofold:

1. The scale is not just in the potential for this happening in a few isolated areas, but across the whole of the Draft Withdrawal Agreement.

2. When adherence to European Union legislation is written into legally-binding text, it becomes harder to argue that this is a voluntary decision of the UK to take note of what the European

Union is doing. It becomes, in practice, an obligation - and that is something else entirely.

I wonder to what extent many Brexiteers simply missed this intention in Theresa May's Mansion House speech.

This wasn't the only area where the UK made unnecessary concessions in terms of our future policy. For example, Theresa May also said this in her Mansion House speech:

As with any trade agreement, we must accept the need for binding commitments - for example, we may choose to commit some areas of our regulations like state aid and competition to remaining in step with the EU's. The UK drove much of the policy in this area and we have much to gain from maintaining proper disciplines on the use of subsidies and on anti-competitive practices.

The problem with EU policy on State Aid is that it gets the balance completely wrong. The procedures are bureaucratic and fail to provide sufficient opportunity for trade defence measures to be taken. We saw this with the closure of SSI in Redcar. The government had to announce an £80 million package to help redundant steel workers caused by the closure, but a little strategic thought would have resulted in a different outcome.

When SSI in Redcar closed, there were many reasons: the strong pound (at the time), China dumping steel below cost price on world markets, high energy prices, etc.

In such situations, it's often appropriate to give State Aid to allow a business which should be profitable to survive a tough time (and when the State Aid is less than the redundancy/unemployment payments the State would have to make if it didn't).

However, Articles 107 and 108 of the Treaty on the Functioning of the European Union prevent the UK from giving such State Aid without the EU Commission's approval. The UK government hid behind that fact, didn't ask for Commission approval, and SSI went under – costing thousands of jobs both directly and in the supply chain. As I said to ITV at the time,

The tragic part is that the plant could have been profitable in the long term; raw materials will not always be so expensive, the pound will not always be so strong and Chinese dumping is not permanent so steel prices will rise.

Whilst in general, I believe state subsidies of business to be a bad thing, there are specific times where it makes strategic common sense to do so. The United Kingdom could, and should, have done more.

The European Union legislation on State Aid was a minor factor in the referendum. Still, the United Kingdom should not voluntarily concede the effective continuation of a system which causes significant problems.

Many Brexiteers attach 100% of the blame for the closure of SSI to the European Union. It's not actually fair for them to do so: there were many factors involved, not least a lack of attention on the part of the UK government.

One area where it is vital for the United Kingdom to diverge from the European Union is public procurement. The UK has a very poor record of such procurement: it often ends up paying too much on contracts with private-sector firms which fail to achieve the stated aims. There is no possibility (especially in marginal cases) for the UK to err on the side of working with British businesses, which create jobs in the UK directly.

Article 75 gives a flavour of just how strongly the UK is likely to be tied in to the European Union under the Withdrawal Agreement:

For the purposes of this Title, "relevant rules" means the general principles of Union law applicable to the award of public contracts, Directives 2009/81/EC, 2014/23/EU, 2014/24/EU and 2014/25/EU of the European Parliament and of the Council, Regulations (EC) No 2195/20025 and (EC) No 1370/20076 of the European Parliament and of the Council, Article 4 of Council Regulation (EEC) No 3577/927, Articles 11 and 12 of Council Directive 96/67/EC, Articles 16, 17 and 18 of Regulation (EC) 1008/2008 of the European Parliament and of the Council, Articles 6 and 7 of Regulation (EU) 2017/352 of the European Parliament and of the Council, and any other specific provisions of Union law governing public procurement procedures.

This is into double figures for the number of pieces of legislation quoted in a single Article of the Withdrawal Agreement. The intention, quite clearly, is to bind the UK's policy as closely as possible to the European Union's. There may, however, be times when the UK wishes to exercise its own sovereign policy on such matters. It is fundamentally wrong, in my view, for the UK to be making long-term concessions about its future actions. The deciders of British government policy should be the British government, not the European Union - especially after Brexit.

What's most concerning about the Draft Withdrawal Agreement is just how restrictive it is. It even makes some concessions which go beyond the current agreements that we have as European Union members, for example on Gibraltar:

In order to prevent and deter the smuggling of products subject to excise duties or special taxes, the United Kingdom shall ensure that, in respect of alcohol and petrol, a tax system which aims at preventing fraudulent activities involving those products is in force in Gibraltar.

In practical terms, this probably means that Spain wants Gibraltar to increase taxes on alcohol and petrol. There is a similar paragraph about tobacco products elsewhere in the Agreement. Whilst there is an argument which can be made that Gibraltar should increase such taxes, this really should not be something that the United Kingdom should be writing into a legally-binding agreement with the European Union. Tax sovereignty is an essential part of sovereignty; Gibraltar's tax system shouldn't be determined by the Withdrawal Agreement.

But amidst everything that is clearly wrong with this draft Withdrawal Agreement, perhaps surprisingly given its length, the biggest question is how much is left unsaid, or hidden, or obfuscated. I've read through the whole text more than once, and I'm still not confident that I've spotted all of the hidden traps within it.

There's quite a lot of technical detail, such as the nature of the Joint Committee to be set up to police the Agreement. Then there's Article 132, which permits an extension of the so-called 'transition period' up to potentially the end of 2022. That would be 6 and a half years after the referendum. The transition period isn't even, really, a transition period in any meaningful sense.

What do you think of when you hear the word transition? I think of a smooth slope from A to B, a gradual change from one arrangement to the next to ensure that everything runs smoothly. But there's nothing gradual about the so-called transitional period. The UK's arrangements with the European Union don't taper over a period of time. This is simply a holding position, until the final deal has been negotiated. It's not a process of slow, gradual change.

The final deal hasn't been agreed. All we have is the 26-page Political Declaration, which describes in general terms what the UK and the European Union are supposedly working towards.

This Political Declaration sets alarm bells ringing in a number of areas:

1. It describes future fishing arrangements which don't seem much

different to the disastrous Common Fisheries Policy.

2. It suggests that the UK will not regain the right to set its own policy on public procurement, allowing the EU to sue the UK if it doesn't agree with UK decisions.

3. Throughout the document, it mentions that questions may be referred to EU courts to determine the meaning of EU law. At first reading, that doesn't seem as bad as it actually is: of course EU courts should interpret EU law, and UK courts should interpret UK law. The kicker, though, is that the UK repeatedly agreed in the Withdrawal Agreement to respecting equivalent standards to EU law. Therefore, EU courts will be able to test the UK's compliance and - in effect - EU courts will overrule UK courts.

4. It raises the spectre of the UK participating in EU-led military missions. In such cases, UK forces would operationally report to EU commanders. Such things might be understandable within NATO, where the UK also takes a leadership role at times, and where a clear pact requires mutual protection. But this is different: this is the UK, as an outsider, potentially contributing to someone else's military force.

5. I'm concerned about the meaning of the wording on development co-operation. Does this mean that the UK is committing to pursuing the same wrong-headed goals with respect to foreign aid that it is doing at present? Does wording elsewhere make it harder for the UK to actually do the things we should be doing instead, to help lift countries out of poverty through free and fair trade rather than

giving handouts with one hand whilst imposing tariffs with the other?

There are many, many more concerns that I have with this document - this is just scratching the surface. The whole thing is lop-sided; it consistently pushes UK requirements to fall into line with the EU rather than being a genuine two-way process. Many mentions of UK co-operating with EU bodies are undefined. They could mean almost anything, including continued erosion of our sovereignty.

It's a nebulous document, with gentle dustings of occasional intermittent sugar-coating. It refers to an 'independent trade policy' for the UK repeatedly, for example. I wonder though: under a document such as this, just how independent could our trade policy actually be?

How could the United Kingdom realistically, under these circumstances, agree the kind of trade deal with a third country that would be beneficial to both sides?

Remember the goods-services issue which I mentioned in previous chapters? The UK needs to be able to offer trade deals to other countries in which we buy goods tariff-free from them, and they buy services freely from us. If our relationship with the European Union means that we can't arrange to take other countries' goods tariff-free, why would those other countries want the deal with us for services?

That's the problem with this deal: whilst we technically regain the ability to negotiate our own trade deals, no country would realistically be able to agree an ambitious trade deal with us.

Worse than this, remember that the Political Declaration is not fully legally binding. It has a lesser status than the Withdrawal Agreement. So whilst the supposedly 'good stuff' for the UK is in the Political Declaration, the Withdrawal Agreement is the binding part.

The press have focused upon one small detail of the Withdrawal Agreement: the backstop. This is indeed *an* important issue, but it is being described as though it is the *only* issue with Theresa May's Agreement. The Government lost a battle with Parliament over this issue already: Parliament required the Government to publish the Attorney General's legal advice regarding the Withdrawal Agreement in relation to the Irish border and backstop question. The legal advice was particularly concerning.

The main problem is that the backstop arrangements are designed to be temporary, but there is no time limit on how long they can last. Whilst they would be mildly uncomfortable to the European Union, they would be hugely uncomfortable to the UK. This would place the UK at a huge disadvantage in the next rounds of negotiations for transposing the Political Declaration into a lasting political agreement after March 29th. Without a time limit, could the United Kingdom potentially be trapped forever in that situation, a situation which many Brexiteers consider to be 'worse than Remain'?

The problem is that there exists no mechanism by which the Agreement can be overturned once it's put in place. There is no 'Article 50 equivalent'. We can't simply give notice that we're intending to leave this Withdrawal Agreement; if ratified, we would be stuck in limbo.

The Attorney General's legal advice is six pages long, but point 16 is particularly instructive:

It is difficult to conclude otherwise than that the Protocol is intended to subsist even when negotiations have clearly broken down. The ordinary meaning of the provisions set out above and considered in their context allows no obvious room for the termination of the Protocol, save by the achievement of an agreement fulfilling the same objectives. Therefore, despite statements in the Protocol that it is not intended to be permanent, and the clear intention of the parties that it should be replaced by alternative, permanent arrangements, in international law the Protocol would endure Indefinitely until a superseding agreement took its place, in whole or in part, as set out therein. Further, the Withdrawal Agreement cannot provide a legal means of compelling the EU to conclude such an agreement.

This is worrying: there is no means of leaving provided for in the Agreement and it's pretty clear that there's not intended to be a means of leaving. This presents a problem because of Article 56 of the Vienna Convention on the Law on Treaties:

A treaty which contains no provision regarding its termination and which does not provide for denunciation or withdrawal is not subject to denunciation or withdrawal unless:

(a) it is established that the parties intended to admit the possibility of denunciation or withdrawal; or

(b) a right of denunciation or withdrawal may be implied by the nature of the treaty.

There is no reasonable legal mechanism for the UK to leave the Withdrawal Agreement. Once ratified, we will be trapped within it - for better or worse.

There's a principle in British law that no Parliament may legally bind its successor. Under this principle, we could have left the European Union prior to the introduction of Article 50 simply by repealing the 1972 European Communities Act. The UK's entry into the European Union (or EEC as then) could only happen subject to the sovereign right of a future Parliament to rip up the Agreement.

Under the Withdrawal Agreement, though, what does tearing up the Agreement actually mean? The Agreement is to leave the European Union. It's difficult to say that we should rip that up; it's not possible to unilaterally reverse the Agreement for leaving the EU and suddenly be back in the EU.

The UK would be stuck in this situation, not just until the end of the 'transition period', but indefinitely until an agreement could be reached on the Irish border issue. The United Kingdom would be putting itself into a position where it could effectively be held to ransom by the European Union. As the Attorney General's legal advice suggests, it's meant to still be binding *even if* negotiations have clearly broken down at some future date. The Attorney General concludes:

In conclusion, the current drafting of the Protocol, including Article 19, does not provide for a mechanism that is likely to enable the UK lawfully to exit the UK wide customs union without a subsequent agreement. This remains the case even if parties are still negotiating many years later, and even if the parties believe that talks have clearly broken down and there is no prospect of a future relationship agreement.

For these reasons, Theresa May has recognised that the deal is unlikely to go through Parliament as it stands. She is seeking appropriate assurances that this permanent limbo situation would not be allowed to occur, though it is far from clear a) that the European Union will agree to it, and b) that such guarantees, unless they actually formed part of the Withdrawal Agreement, would afford the UK legally-binding protection under the law.

The backstop issue is clearly of key legal importance, but I fear that the focus solely on this one issue is causing the other issues with Theresa May's Agreement to be brushed under the carpet. This is a very worrying state of affairs.

The Attorney General's legal advice covers the backstop. What has not been published is the corresponding legal advice for the rest of the Withdrawal Agreement? What traps might be lurking in the rest of the advice, which neither we nor the MPs who will be voting on it shortly are yet aware of?

Having said all of this, it does seem that the UK will - by and large - regain control over its immigration system under Theresa May's deal. The so-called 'free movement' will end, and eventually (but not until after the 'transition period') the UK will start to regain that control.

Between the Agreement being reached and published, I wrote that I would judge the Agreement on the following questions - by the end of the process, will we have:

1. Stopped EU courts overruling our own?
2. Repatriated legislative power from Brussels to Westminster?
3. Stopped sending vast sums of money to the EU each year?
4. Gained the ability to sign our own free trade deals, without EU rules interfering with our trading arrangements with other nations?
5. Regained full control over our policy on immigration, ending the discrimination between EU and non-EU immigration?
6. Regained full control over our sovereign waters and fisheries?

1. EU courts will overrule our own in practice, but not in theory.
2. We will regain some legislative power, but having agreed to keep our policies aligned with the EU's in so many areas, we won't fully regain that power. During the 'transition period', the situation will be even worse.
3. We'll still be paying huge sums of money to the European Union each year until after the transition period. There are no guarantees in the Political Declaration that there won't be further financial commitments asked of the UK as part of the future relationship.

4. Whilst we technically regain the ability to sign our own trade deals, the mechanics of the Agreement makes it somewhat improbable that any meaningful agreements could be signed.

5. We would regain most of our immigration policy, though not quite all.

6. It seems likely that the UK will not regain full control over our waters and fisheries.

From this point of view, I feel that Theresa May's deal is a disaster overall. There is one reason, and one reason alone, why anyone might support it: immigration.

The Remain caricature of Brexiteers suggests that Brexit supporters are obsessed about immigration to the detriment of all else. It seems to me that Theresa May has negotiated with that principle in mind - failing to understand the fuller range of motivations of Brexit voters.

If you are indeed a Brexiteer who cares solely about ending our current quasi-racist immigration system which discriminates in favour of the overwhelmingly-white EU27 and against the ethnically-diverse rest of the world, then you might well find May's deal to be to your liking. It delivers upon that. The problem is that it delivers upon little, if anything, else.

CHAPTER 15

THE CONSERVATIVE LEADERSHIP COUP

On December 12th 2018, the Conservative backbench MPs finally put in a motion of no confidence in Theresa May. Brexiteers from a variety of political parties had been calling for such a motion for many months previously. This meant that 48 Conservative MPs (i.e. 15% of the total Parliamentary Party) would have to write letters to Sir Graham Brady, the Chairman of the 1922 Committee.

I'd written previously that it would be a mistake to submit the 48 letters too soon: as part of the Conservative Party's arcane rules, if such a motion were to fail to get the support of the majority of MPs, Theresa May would be immune from any further challenge for 12 months. Such a motion should only be submitted in the event that it would be realistically winnable, or in a situation so utterly dire that there was literally no other choice: it had to be tried.

When the 'Chequers' proposals were made, which would form the eventual basis for Theresa May's letters, 48 letters did not go in.
September passed, and the 48 letters did not go in.
October passed, and the 48 letters did not go in.
In November, the Withdrawal Agreement was published. The 48 letters did not go on.

There were rumours of letters, MPs claiming in public that they'd sent letters (even though they hadn't), MPs claiming in public that they'd not sent letters (even though they had), and MPs publishing the text of the letters they'd sent - to prove that they were telling the truth about the letters they'd sent.

In all of the consequent media circus, the strong Brexiteer Conservative MPs were being made a laughing stock in the press. Couldn't they even muster 48 letters? How impotent Tory backbenchers and the ERG must be, hinted the headlines, if they couldn't get 48 MPs to support them.

Getting the 48 letters wasn't the problem though. It was the motion of no confidence. Around the publication of the Withdrawal Agreement, I wrote on my Facebook page as follows:

I want a change in Prime Minister. Now let's pause and take stock for a moment. Which of these two scenarios is most likely to achieve that?

A: 48 letters
B: Parliament votes down the Withdrawal Agreement

If A, then the question is whether they can get the 158 (or so) votes needed to defeat May in a moon of no confidence. My gut feeling is that they can't: if 48 signatures are difficult, 158 votes may be more so. In that case, we're literally toast. May will be safe from leadership challenge for another year.

As for B, well Parliament is going to vote this deal down..under such circumstances, she's much more likely to be toast than if 48 letters go in now.

With apologies for the double-use of a grilled-bread-related metaphor, this was always the worry. Every time I saw an MP put in a letter, I was conflicted: I approved of their intentions, but not necessarily of their strategy.

In the first week of December, after the government had been found in contempt of Parliament over the publication of the Attorney General's legal advice, something which had never before happened to a UK government, 48 letters still did not go in.

When Theresa May cancelled the pre-Christmas vote on the Withdrawal Agreement, with talk of a motion of no confidence in the government itself - something which could lead to a General Election - the threshold of 48 letters was finally reached. The problem? The ticking clock would potentially remove the Canada option from the table completely.

The Conservative backbench MPs had been backed into a corner. The Prime Minister had been humiliated by a House of Commons in which she had been attacked from all sides. With hindsight, the decision to pull the trigger on the 48 letters may still have been a premature one.

For Conservative MPs to evict a sitting Prime Minister is no small matter under their internal rules. At any given time, there are roughly 140 MPs who are either Ministers or Parliamentary Private Secretaries. This is known as the 'payroll vote': they are expected to either support the Government, or resign their positions.

There were 318 Conservative MPs at the time: they could only win a motion of no confidence if a) much of the 'payroll vote' supported it, or b) the backbench MPs were almost unanimous in supporting it.

The motion of no confidence was held quickly. The timescale was condensed into a single day, with little time for speculation or campaigning. MPs had to make a snap decision, with Theresa May gaining the opportunity to address the 1922 Committee before the decision was taken. It gave May's opponents little chance to do anything, and the result was 200-117 in favour of the Prime Minister. Whilst a majority of non-payroll vote MPs had undoubtedly wanted Theresa May gone, the result was clear enough. As her supporters gleefully pointed out, 63% to 37% was more than the 52% to 48% in support of Brexit. Colleagues should 'respect the vote', they said.

Theresa May might have been weakened in the public eye, but in surviving this vote she became immune from further challenge for a year.

Another potential outcome had been removed from the table. Supposing that there had been a Conservative leadership election in December, a new Prime Minister would just about have had time to explore genuine alternatives to Theresa May's Withdrawal Agreement.

Essentially, both the Norway option and the Canada option became unrealistic on that day. As the clock continued to tick, the options continued to narrow. If it was a strategy by Theresa May, it was a high-risk strategy. It represented her only hope of getting the Withdrawal Agreement through Parliament. The deal was now completely associated with Theresa May. This was no longer a Conservative Party deal, or a Government deal. It was now simply Theresa May's deal.

If you've ever watched Game of Thrones, one way of looking at Season 6 and the early part of Season 7 is that they killed off the characters who would not form part of the final series. They made sure that the remaining characters were the ones needed to finish the story. By streamlining the action, they prepared the finale.

The 48 letters and the failed Conservative leadership coup is reminiscent of that. Three options (Norway; Canada; an involuntary change of Conservative Prime Minister) were removed on December 12th, 2018.

A very good way of understanding the situation we find ourselves in today, in January 2019, is to see the last few months as precisely that: politicians working to narrow the list of choices for their own ends.

CHAPTER 16

THE NO-DEAL SCENARIO
(AND IS IT REALLY 'CRASHING OUT'?)

There's a lot of nonsense, on all sides, talked about a no-deal Brexit. This is because it is, in essence, the purist's version of Brexit. For those who wanted to Remain in the European Union, it is the stuff of nightmares. For those who wanted to Leave, it is the one way of guaranteeing that Brexit will actually be delivered on. This has led to a string of ridiculous claims made on both sides.

There is, in fact, a logical problem with the possibility of the final outcome being no-deal. I wrote about this in an article for the Burkean back in September, before Theresa May's deal had been finalised. I said that Remain (with or without a second referendum), a deal based upon Chequers (essentially, the Theresa May deal), or the Norway option, all suffer from a difficult situation: there is no majority for it in Parliament, and there is at least one key player in the whole thing which considers it worse than no-deal. I argued that what we've seen for the last two years is jockeying for position, with each group trying to persuade the others not to veto their preferred option.

I wrote about Game Theory and the Prisoner's Dilemma, the film A Beautiful Mind and how John Nash was able to apply these principles to explain all kinds of real-world situations including nuclear deterrence. I argued that we should be asking a different question: given that no-deal is the default position in law, is there a 'strategy' which dominates a no-deal scenario? If there's an alternative that the vast majority of people and politicians would all prefer to no-deal, then it's difficult to imagine how no-deal could be the eventual outcome.

The idea of a simple free-trade deal between the UK and the European Union, as described in the previous chapter, fits the bill. Even most people who support a pure, clean Brexit would have little problem with avoiding tariffs on imports and exports between the UK and the EU. Whilst most Remainers would dislike it, they would dislike it less than they would dislike a no-deal Brexit.

In Game Theory terms, we say that a free-trade deal strategy *dominates* a no-deal strategy. There's no reason to stick to no-deal when it's possible for everyone to be happier by shifting from that to a simple free trade deal instead. If you'd asked me back in September, I would have suggested that the scenario described in the previous chapter might therefore be much more likely than most people thought.

Since then, the clock has been ticking. Four months later, Theresa May has done nothing quite so effectively as she has played for time. In the meantime, an attempted coup amongst her own backbenchers to remove her as Prime Minister has failed. It seems fairly clear that Theresa May is unwilling to negotiate a fundamentally different kind of future relationship with the European Union to that which she has already agreed.

Even if there is a strong logical reason to suppose that no-deal is an outcome which shouldn't happen, the only other logically stronger option has a problem of its own: it is becoming increasingly difficult to see how it is possible to arrive at that situation given the amount of time remaining.

Discussion of no-deal has been remarkably poor, even as far as the standards of modern political debate are concerned. It's been a combination of wild, ridiculous claims on the one hand, and absolute denial that any practical problems could be caused on the other. We've seen wild economic claims of doom, and wild economic claims that a no-deal Brexit is some kind of get-rich-quick scheme.

My own view is this: a no-deal Brexit would cause significant problems for a few months. Those problems shouldn't be trivialised, but they shouldn't be sensationalised either. The benefits of Brexit would not be instant, but they would be huge in the longer term. I consider a no-deal Brexit to be the exchange of a few months of pain for decades of prosperity, provided that our politicians are determined to take the actions necessary to achieve that long-term prosperity.

To take one example, the sensationalist headlines suggest that planes would not continue to fly in the event of a no-deal Brexit. Whilst these claims are complete, total and utter baloney, there would be some genuine issues with aviation in the event of a no-deal Brexit.

There was never the slightest chance that an aviation agreement wouldn't happen to permit planes continuing to fly, not least because almost every route out of the Republic of Ireland would require flying over the UK's airspace. The European Commission has now announced its no-deal planning as regards aviation, and it has stated as follows:

- *As regards traffic rights, the Commission "will propose measures to ensure that UK carriers are allowed to fly over the territory of the EU, make technical stops (eg, refuelling without embarkation/ disembarkation of passengers), as well as land in the EU and fly back to the UK", subject to reciprocal treatment of EU carriers by the UK.*
- *As regards safety, the Commission will propose measures to ensure the continued validity of UK type certificates and organisation approvals for a limited period, subject to reciprocal treatment by the UK, and that parts and appliances placed on the EU market before the withdrawal date based on a certificate issued by a person certified by the UK CAA may still be used under certain circumstances.*
- *As regards security, the Commission will take action to ensure that passengers and their cabin baggage flying from the UK and transiting through EU airports continue to be exempted from a second security screening at EU airports.*

That sounds pretty clear, and it is. What it doesn't do, is replicate all of the current agreements which the UK and the EU have in terms of flying planes.

Across the world, aviation is based upon the so-called 'five freedoms'. The no-deal planning suggests that we'll still have the first four of these between the UK and the European Union. We won't have the fifth: the ability to fly between two different EU countries and pick up passengers before returning to the UK. We won't have some of the extended aviation agreements - for example, the right for a UK airline to operate a flight between France and Germany irrespective of whether or not that plane is subsequently coming back to the United Kingdom.

In the event of a no-deal Brexit, the permissions lost would cause some disruption to air travel, at the expense of both British carriers and other EU carriers. The truth, in this case, is that there would be some disruption. That disruption would be significant, but not apocalyptic.

I've used aviation as just one example of many. I could have discussed arrangements at ports (yes, it would result in additional queues at the border, but no, it wouldn't result in the kind of utter chaos and catastrophe that we're being threatened with in some quarters). We could go on, sector by sector. No, there isn't a danger that the UK won't be able to import life-saving medicines. No, the UK isn't going to suddenly be unable to import enough food to feed our population. Would no-deal result in changes to suppliers, though? Yes, it probably would in some cases. Would some goods become more expensive in the short-term if we had tariffs? Yes. Would exports to the EU become harder under a tariff regime? Yes. On the other hand, such a regime would lead to substantial extra revenue to the Exchequer which could offset some of those costs in one way or another.

I'm always wary of suggesting that bringing in income through tariffs is a good thing though: it hurts the economy to do it. It can, however, benefit specific businesses. Suppose that you're a small town in America with a steel mill in your town. If America imposes tariffs upon the import of steel, that's great for your local steel mill. It is easier for that mill to sell to other businesses across America, because it suddenly finds that it's much more competitive.

So it's great for American business, then? Wrong. Because those businesses which require steel will now have to pay higher prices to buy the same steel. It will put prices up. It will cost jobs because prices have to increase. Consumers will pay more for end products. It's great for that one sector of American manufacturing. It's great for the town that's especially reliant upon the steel industry. But it's bad for the economy as a whole.

Now, there are times when it's appropriate to introduce tariffs regardless. For example, when China started selling steel on global markets at (effectively) below the cost of production, this would lead to other countries' steel industries struggling and losing business. Once enough of them were eliminated, China could stop subsidising steel and increase prices. This would cause a long-term problem for other nations. That's why tariffs can be used as a defensive measure: yes, they do cause harm - but they might be necessary as a means to prevent a greater harm.

Trade on World Trade Organisation terms would mean sector-by-sector tariffs between the UK and the EU. Whilst they would average around 3%, some sectors have higher tariffs. A tariff of around 10% on cars might be problematic for German car manufacturers, but it would also not be ideal for manufacturers based in the UK either. There would also be technical problems: if you're importing components used in the manufacture, there are limits to what percentage you're allowed to import if you're then going to export the item. I'm paraphrasing and oversimplifying here, a lot, but the principle does actually matter. A no-deal Brexit would cause significant problems for business, over and above the tariffs.

These issues are more than a mild annoyance. It would probably trigger a recession in the UK. There would be, I suspect, around 6 months of very difficult economic times.

In the event of a no-deal Brexit, the pound would fall further on foreign exchange markets. This would make British goods more attractive and boost British manufacturing.

The UK would be in a free, unencumbered position to negotiate trade deals. Every negative relating to the European Union could, in time, be counterbalanced by a positive relating to non-EU countries. Over time, it would be very surprising if the UK did not negotiate at the very least a tariff-free trade deal with the European Union. I am convinced that, within a couple of years, the UK would be able to demonstrate significant benefits from Brexit.

What about the economic projections that the UK would be worse off in the event of a no-deal Brexit?

First of all, we need to be careful that we're talking about the same thing. The Bank of England performs 'shock tests' on economic scenarios, designed to check how resilient the economy would be in the event of the worst-case scenario occurring. Those aren't economic predictions, but contingency planning. There's a huge difference between the two.

That being said, there have been various economic models which do seem to suggest that the UK would be worse off in the event of a no-deal Brexit. Some economists (notably Patrick Minford) offer a dissenting voice, suggesting that the UK would eventually benefit. Those reports which suggest a negative prognosis for the economy generally have six failings in common:

1. They assume the EU will remain as it is today, failing to count the economic cost of anticipated changes in EU policy

2. Their modelling techniques underestimate 'added value' arising from Brexit

3. There is evidence of groupthink within most modelling techniques, leading to duplication of effort as well as potential duplication of errors

4. No modelling technique takes account of potential economic gains which could be made as a result of extra policy options provided to governments post-Brexit

5. They work on a measure of GDP rather than GDP per capita

6. Reports are often misquoted, leading to headline claims in newspapers which don't match the actual reports.

We've already covered 1 in a previous chapter, discussing such things as the proposed Financial Transaction Tax, the Common Consolidated Corporate Tax base, the costs of additional EU regulations expected in the coming years, environmental policies, and the projected increase to the European Union budget.

The second isn't necessarily an easy failure for economic models to be able to correct: some of the most likely benefits of Brexit are difficult to measure. It is difficult to know precisely which EU legislation a government would repeal following Brexit, and even more difficult to know *when* it would finally get around to it. Modelling this is therefore problematic. What is clear is that the UK would, in the event of a no-deal Brexit, gain the ability to set its own rules to apply to businesses which do not trade with the EU27.

The benefits of doing this would apply to:

- Businesses which trade only within the United Kingdom
- Businesses which trade with non-EU countries
- Businesses which, although trading with the EU27, do the majority of their business either within the UK or outside the EU

We should recall that the categories I've just mentioned represent well over 90% of the UK economy. Trade with the European Union represents under 10% of the UK economy. Therefore, any benefit to the 90%+ should be treated seriously.

There are many different approaches which could be taken by a British government to reduce the regulatory burden. These will be unique on a sectoral basis: for example in the field of transport, it should be possible to streamline current rules on permitted hours for lorry drivers, which are badly drafted and lead to considerable difficulties within the haulage industry. In medicine, reform of the Clinical Trials Directive could reverse recent loss in research. We would be able to proceed with reform of EU insolvency law, and to deal with issues such as double compliance with UK/EU standards.

There exists a certain irony in that there is much discussion of non-tariff barriers when it comes to EU-UK relations post Brexit, despite an already close alignment of legislation, but when it comes to the negotiation of trade deals between the UK and third countries, the advantages of breaking down non-tariff barriers as well as the direct impact of a trade deal is often neglected.

It is worth noting that the balance of the UK's trade is likely to change post-Brexit. Yes, under the current system, the UK does about 46% of its trade with the EU27. But that figure is only so high because the current system is biased towards trade with the EU. In a more neutral system, it's quite likely that the UK would do more trade with non-EU countries than it does at present. In any event, that is likely to be the case as the world's growth markets are not generally other EU nations. The EU economy is declining quickly as a proportion of world trade.

One example of the failure of such economic models to consider the impact of Brexit is that many fail to project any economic benefit at all from the recovery of the British fishing industry. Yet this is one area where the UK has the ability to guarantee control over her own resources, and therefore to rebuild fishing fleets without risking overfishing or conservation issues.

The third common error was 'groupthink' amongst these models. One of the features of much of the available research is that it refers to previous research, not providing independent new data but recombining existing data in a different way. This is, of course, cost-effective from the point of view of producing a projection, but it runs the risk of circular reasoning. Indeed, many studies use a 'meta-study' approach, taking the average of all available projections. The problem here is that the average of all available projections will naturally ensure that further projections hold to similar inbuilt bias.

Whether a 'gravity model' or 'classical model' is used for trade projections has a considerable impact. If it should transpire that the gravity model is better, then the majority of the literature would prove broadly correct (at least, were it not for the other factors raised in this paper). But if it were to emerge that a classical approach fits the data more effectively, then Professor Minford (et al) would likely prove to be correct.

A gravity model essentially places greater weight upon geographical proximity. Irrespective of which model has been most appropriate in the past, it is certainly arguable that as technology improves - breaking down geographical barriers - that even if the gravity model had been preferable in recent years, the classical model may rightly make a comeback.

I wrote a paper on the subject of economic projections and Brexit which goes into much more detail on the specific reasoning behind believing that one model or the other might be more accurate, which can be downloaded from my website. For here, suffice it to say that the 'groupthink' mentality leaves open a substantial rationale for believing that all the models might be wrong in the same direction. This would also explain the failure of Treasury and other projections in predicting what would happen to the British economy in the immediate aftermath of a Leave vote.

I believe it's the failure of those projections which has contributed to the huge chasm in public opinion when it comes to so-called expert analysis. I don't believe for a moment that there is a huge percentage of the population which would discount genuine expert opinion on any subject. We wouldn't generally take the word of friends and family above that of a lawyer on legal issues. We wouldn't ask the bloke down the pub to diagnose medical symptoms; we'd go to a doctor. But the problem with economics is that it is a bit more nebulous; predictions have to be taken with a pinch of salt because it depends upon so many complex factors. When economics has been misused in the past, to create a false air of authority, can we really be surprised that people then reject more of the same? It has become so easy for people to simply believe whichever side agrees with their own opinion, rather than to think for themselves.

Fourthly, economic models cannot easily (and certainly do not really attempt in practice to) project what a government might do with its new-found freedom to legislate in the best interests of the

UK rather than compromise in the interests of the EU27. Here, again, it's difficult to criticise the economic models themselves because there is a certain amount of guesswork in ascertaining what a government, independent of Brussels, would actually do. Some of these suggestions simply aren't covered by the economic modelling; I won't go into detail but the potential for added-value on leaving the European Union is clear:

a) The potential to replace VAT with a less bureaucratic system, with the consequent reduction to regulatory burdens on business, and virtually eliminating the VAT fraud which costs the British economy billions of pounds every year.

b) The ability to replace EU funding with targeted alternatives across a range of policy areas: agriculture, regional development, etc.

c) The ability to ignore EU economic rules - the UK would never have ended up with the costly public-private partnership schemes under Blair if it had not been for European Union rules, for example.

d) The ability of the UK to legislate or vary taxes in different areas (I'm thinking of fuel duty, VAT on hot food, business regulations, and so on.

e) Potential boosts to the UK economy caused by no longer being bound by the EU Procurement Directive.

f) As discussed in the previous chapter, the ability to give state aid in targeted circumstances without first seeking the approval of the

European Commission.

g) The ability for the UK to employ its own anti-dumping measures and other trade defence mechanisms.

The cumulative impact of all of this could be substantial, but it isn't ever really considered.

Fifthly, the use of GDP rather than GDP per-capita skews the projections substantially. The average person, thinking about how well off they'll be, is considering their own income. They're not thinking about the aggregate size of the UK economy. The UK's economy is far bigger than Singapore's, but the average person in Singapore earns far more than the average person in the UK. We can hardly gloat and say 'our economy is bigger' when the fact is simply that the UK has a population of over 60 million; Singapore's is under 6 million.

When you drill down into the detail of these economic projections, they suggest that the population would be lower under a no-deal Brexit than in a base-case Remain scenario. This difference, of between 1 million and 2 million people, accounts for at the very least a couple of percent of GDP - and possibly more.

Finally, headline writers often gold-plate a study, assuming that the absolute worst-case scenario found by a model is the one that's going to happen. This contributes to the suspicion of economic experts which has been a symptom of recent developments on Brexit.

The media have used emotive phrases such as 'crashing out' or 'a cliff-edge' when it comes to the potential for a no-deal Brexit. This has even been the case with the purportedly-impartial BBC.

A fair, sensible view of a no-deal Brexit is probably somewhere between what both sides seem to be claiming at present. It wouldn't be a disaster, but it would cause short-term problems. It would offer the potential for substantial long-term gains, but that would be in turn dependent upon the government being prepared to take the necessary advantages to prove some 'value-added' from Brexit.

We should not fear a no-deal Brexit, but those who are desperately seeking a no-deal Brexit should do so with their eyes wide open. It is not an ideal solution, but if forced to choose between Theresa May's deal and a no-deal Brexit, I would choose the latter.

Why? Because in the words of Theresa May, ***No deal is better than a bad deal***. Perhaps she no longer believes that. Perhaps she never did.

CHAPTER 17

WHAT WOULD A SECOND REFERENDUM LOOK LIKE?

The simple answer: a second referendum would be absolute chaos. Those seeking to overturn Brexit have suggested that holding another referendum would be a means by which the clock could be turned back to where we were in early 2016, before the referendum. It's generally a suggestion based upon a desire: their desire to overturn the result of the referendum that we've already had. I won't talk too much about the rationale behind the request for another referendum in this chapter, but instead I'm going to look at the practicalities of it.

It's easy for campaigners to want a second referendum, but it's harder for Parliament to force one. The practical obstacles lead to one inescapable conclusion:

 If a second referendum happens, it will be rushed.

1. A second referendum requires legislation to go through Parliament

For a referendum to happen, an Act of Parliament would have to be passed requiring one. It's clear that there would be huge opposition to this in the House of Commons, and there would probably also be some (but lesser) opposition in the House of Lords. It is just about possible for an Act of Parliament to be passed in three weeks, if the

Government allocates sufficient Parliamentary time for it to happen. This is incredibly rare, and hasn't happened since 2005 when the Prevention of Terrorism Act was passed.

2. A second referendum requires a Government committed to holding a second referendum

Even if they had the Parliamentary numbers to push through a second referendum, the Opposition would be unable to force this through: the Government wouldn't allocate the time for it. Could Theresa May really recommend a second referendum, given that this would absolutely split her own political party? I doubt it. But for another Prime Minister to take over would require even more delays.

3. The law requires a minimum 10-week campaign period for any referendum

The Political Parties, Elections and Referendums Act (PPERA) describes how a campaign period for a referendum works. This includes a 4-week period during which there is time for campaigns to apply to be designated as the 'official' campaign on each side. There is then a 2-week period, during which the Electoral Commission decides who should be designated as the 'official' campaigns. Following that, there is a 4-week period for the campaign proper.

For a 10-week campaign period to happen, with polling day being Thursday March 28th (the day before the referendum), the legislation would have to be passed and receive Royal Assent by Thursday

January 17th at the latest. Given the date when people are likely to be reading this book, that could prove to be somewhat problematic!

4. The Electoral Commission is supposed to assess the referendum question

The process of doing this lasts for 12 weeks. It's supposed to include such things as public consultations, and campaigners on both sides, before feeding this back to Parliament so that Parliament can determine the question. In order to have a second referendum, the 12-week period would have to be condensed and happen after the legislation had been passed for the referendum itself.

Parliament would literally have to legislate *subject to* the Electoral Commission's later advice on what the question should be. This would be a mind-boggling state of affairs.

5. Parliament would have to completely overrule the Electoral Commission's advice on funding for referendums

After the referendum on AV in 2011 (the UK had a referendum on changing the voting system from the not-proportional First Past The Post system to another not-proportional Alternative Vote system), the Electoral Commission demanded that there must be at least 6 months prior to polling day to sort out the funding. As Jenny Watson, Chair of the Electoral Commission and Chief Counting Officer at the 2011 referendum on AV, said:

The Government should also accept and implement the principle of agreeing funding legislation for polls by six months before polling day – rather than just 4 ½ weeks in this case- to allow for proper planning.

6. To do otherwise would require the repeal of the Act of Parliament governing referendums

This, I think, is a non-starter. If Parliament were to repeal or amend the Act of Parliament which governs elections and referendums, solely to change the timescale for one specific referendum, I suspect that there would be a level of outcry beyond that which we can reasonably imagine at present. A second change in the law might also add to the Parliamentary time required to pass the legislation.

We can safely rule this idea out. Therefore..

7. The European Union would have to agree to extend Article 50

Even if all of the above were to happen, on short timescales, with the Electoral Commission advice being completely ignored, there is still a minimum of 13 weeks (3 weeks for the passage of an Act of Parliament; 10 weeks for the statutory referendum timescale). The deadline for achieving that before March 29th was before Christmas 2018. That ship has now sailed.

8. But the European Union won't extend Article 50 beyond the end of June 2019 without a very good reason

What I'm about to say may surprise you. The European Union does not want a second referendum on Brexit as much as you might think.

A second referendum isn't a good enough reason for them to be willing to extend Article 50 for another six months or so.

There are European elections in May. Those European elections will determine who is in the European Parliament. Thanks to the so-called 'Spitzenkandidaten' process, they will offer the post of President of the European Commission to someone from the pan-European party/grouping which does best in the European elections in May.

The new European Parliament and Commission must be in place by July 2019. When the UK leaves the European Union, the number of seats which each country gets in the European Parliament changes. They've already planned and prepared for each country having additional seats from July.

> **If the UK doesn't take part in the European elections in May, then decides to Remain in the EU anyway, the European Union has a serious problem. Its entire system of government gets messed up.**

The key date is July 2nd, the date that the new European Parliament sits for the first time and the process of rubber-stamping the new European Commission begins. Brexit must be sorted by then, at least from the EU's perspective.

The European Union would probably, on balance, still like the United Kingdom to reverse Brexit and stay in the EU. It would be midlly useful for them to say things like '*Of course it's unrealistic for you to leave the EU, just look at what happened when Britain tried to leave'* to any other countries which fail to toe the EU line. They might feel that some bridges had been burnt between the EU and the UK, but on balance the feeling tends to be that they would prefer it if Brexit were reversed. That's a lukewarm preference now, though. It's no longer an absolute determination. If they were determined to keep the UK in the EU at any costs, don't you think they'd have tried to offer some sort of 'carrot' to keep the UK in? They haven't. They'd like the UK to stay, but they're more focused on maintaining their own rules, structures and institutions intact. If they had to choose (for example) between their Four Freedoms and having the UK remain in the EU, they'd choose their Four Freedoms.

The European Union are very much focused on their own institutions. People in the UK rarely seem to grasp this: they're fixated on (for example) who the President of the Commission is. Just because we're not too bothered, doesn't mean that they're not bothered either! To the EU and many of its Member States, those questions are very important.

Can you imagine the chaos which would be caused if British uncertainty over Brexit happened whilst the EU was trying to hold a set of European elections, messing up elections in 27 other countries at the same time? The European Union won't agree to that easily. For that reason, they will want a clear decision on what happens next with Brexit by May - at the latest! Even that would be problematic: imagine campaigning in elections where you don't know how many seats there are going to be.

Worse still, what would happen on July 2nd if the UK hadn't left? Would we have gone through another set of European elections in May? How could such elections be called at such short notice? Wouldn't those elections be happening right in the middle of a referendum period which might well confirm that those elections shouldn't be held at all? The whole thing would be full of Kafka-esque surrealism. It would make zero sense.

9. If there were a second referendum, there would need to be time to implement the result of it

Suppose that a second referendum were to back a deal (like Theresa May's) negotiated between the UK and the European Union. In such a case, that deal would still need to be ratified by the European Union. Those constitutional processes require (amongst other things) the European Parliament to sit to ratify such a deal.

But the European Parliament sits for the last time before the European elections on April 18th. After that date, whilst MEPs are still technically in office, they've all gone back to their countries to campaign in the European elections to try to hold onto their seats. Recalling the European Parliament during an election to vote on a Brexit deal wouldn't be particularly straightforward. It would also politicise that vote. What would happen if MEPs, trying to gain more votes for their parties back home, decided to vote against the deal at that point?

Another related question is whether a second referendum would necessarily provide sufficient clarity. We don't know whether the legislation would be drafted in such a way as to make it binding on Parliament and the Government. If there were a second Leave vote, would all Remain opposition to Brexit immediately disappear? If it were to go to Remain, wouldn't Leave campaigners decry the contortions of the process which had produced such a result - and claim that the second referendum had been completely unfair?

10. Therefore, a second referendum would have to happen a lot quicker than people think

We're not talking here about a relaxed timetable even if the European Union were willing to extend Article 50 'a bit'. The UK might easily be able to extend Article 50 for a few weeks, but a few months would be problematic - it would be one thing if that were done with a specific goal in mind, but quite another if it weren't clear what was going to happen next.

This takes us back to the 13-week timescale. A second referendum requires, whatever is done to expedite the process, a minimum of 13 weeks from a Government deciding to hold one and polling day. Even 13 weeks is pushing it massively.

Thirteen weeks from January 17th is April 18th - the last day the European Parliament sits. The results wouldn't even be known by the time the European Parliament rises for elections. The day after that is Good Friday...

Five weeks after that, it's polling day in those elections. For the UK to take part in such elections would - again - require a decision to be made. The level of fudge required to make this happen would be absolutely unprecedented.

But let's suppose that these obstacles somehow vanished. There's another problem with a second referendum:

What would the choices be?

As far as I can see, there are three options which could conceivably be put to the people in a second referendum. The Norway option, the Canada option, and other deals which haven't yet been negotiated, would be difficult to put to the British people because they would require time for negotiation. The only three plausible options which could take any meaningful time at all for public deliberation at this stage would be:

- To overturn the 2016 referendum and Remain in the EU
- To ratify Theresa May's deal
- To leave the European Union without a deal

Which two of these three would be chosen? The so-called 'People's Vote' campaign (an odd phrase, given that those who voted in the 2016 vote were people) would like any referendum with Remain on the ballot paper.

Theresa May would no doubt insist that her deal should be on the ballot paper. Yet, if she were no longer Prime Minister at the time that the decision was taken to hold a referendum, there is a possibility that there would be a move to offer a choice between

Remain and No Deal.

Brexiteers would argue that the people were told in 2016 that the referendum was a 'once in a lifetime' decision and that the government would implement the people's decision. To do otherwise would erode trust in the very foundations of democracy. Brexiteers would further point out that the Remain campaign at the time of the 2016 referendum used the fact that this was a once-in-a-lifetime decision as a campaigning point to seek a Remain vote!

Brexiteers would no doubt argue that there shouldn't be another referendum - but that *if* there were, **then** another referendum would need to ask a fresh question, to adduce further information. They might well accept a question along the lines of '*Britain voted to leave the European Union in 2016. Would you like to leave according to Theresa May's deal, or with no deal?*'

Under such circumstances, there is likely to be wild disagreement about any question. A referendum with three choices would make no sense at all: no option would gain 50% of the vote, and then the interpretation of the result would be difficult. Suppose that Remain 'won' with 35% of the vote, with No Deal and May's Deal getting 33% and 32%. Brexiteers would immediately point out that 65% had supported a Leave option. But if No Deal won with 35% of the vote, Remainers would say that 65% were completely unhappy with it.

A two-part question would suffer from similar problems. 'Do you still want to leave the EU, and if so, would you prefer May's deal or no deal?' would be pretty confusing, and such confusion would be very unhelpful. People might vote tactically on the first question in order to avoid a disliked option on the second question. The outcome of the whole process might be different depending on the way the questions were asked. You could still decide between the same three choices by asking a two-part question like 'Do you accept/reject the Withdrawal Agreement?' and then if people reject it, 'Would you like to leave the EU with no deal, or Remain in the EU?'. Every option would be criticised; it's doubtful whether there would be even the remotest agreement over what the question should be!

And if all that weren't complicated enough...

Remember that every moment spent navigating this maze of options is a moment less remaining for the final decisions to be made about what happens regarding Brexit. If Parliament were so busy legislating for a second referendum in a hurry, there'd suddenly be another piece of legislation which would require their attention at the same time.

For the UK to have a second referendum would mean extending Article 50, but the withdrawal date of March 29th 2019 is currently enshrined in law. Parliament would need to legislate to extend that period, just as the UK would have to receive the permission of the EU27 for the same extension to take place.

The notion of a second referendum is absolutely fraught with difficulties. Those advocating one should seriously consider what it is they're actually asking for. In 2016, when the UK held the original referendum on our membership of the European Union, we had a year to prepare for that referendum. To hold another referendum in such a hurry would throw up all kinds of new issues, and I suspect that whichever side were to win, it would add little to the legitimacy of the course of action.

In the words of political commentator David Herdson,

The idea that because parliament can't decide, the matter should be referred back to the people only makes sense if the people have a clear preference (which they don't), if there is a simple binary choice to be made (there isn't), and if parliament is determined to implement the public decision, which if it was it wouldn't need to ask them in the first place.

Politics in 2019 has become so strange that I wouldn't like to rule anything out altogether, but it seems to me that the notion of a second referendum is particularly fanciful.

There is only one mechanism by which another referendum could easily happen, and that would - I think - be a step too far even for a Remain-supporting Parliament. If the UK were to revoke its Article 50 notification, and then hold a second referendum about whether to begin the whole process again, they would 'gain' another two years.

I suspect that any government supporting such a notion would experience significant difficulties if it were want to be re-elected at any future date!

CHAPTER 18

WHAT HAPPENS NEXT?

"Once you have eliminated the impossible, whatever remains, no matter how improbable, must be the truth" - Sherlock Holmes

When Sir Arthur Conan Doyle wrote those words more than a century ago, he clearly wasn't referring to Brexit. It seems as though working out what's going to happen with Brexit is even more difficult. Every single possibility seems to be not just improbable, but politically impossible.

Give me any possible scenario for what will happen over the next few months, and I can tell you exactly why it's ridiculous.

The notion of the government unilaterally overturning the referendum result and its own legislation? Preposterous.

A second referendum can't happen in time, as we discussed in the last chapter, and there's no reasonable mechanism by which Brexit could be delayed long enough for that anyway.

What about Theresa May's Withdrawal Agreement? It's opposed by at least two-thirds of all MPs. There is no majority in the House of Commons for it, let alone to pass the subsequent legislation that would be needed.

Could the EU back down over the backstop, and that catapult

Theresa May's deal through the Commons? It seems unlikely: the European Union has been digging its heels in on that one for many months without the slightest softening in language.

Could the whole backstop issue be a choreographed charade, designed for the EU to back down at the eleventh hour and set a deadline? It seems unlikely (though many Brexiteers suspect that could happen), but even if the backstop issue were resolved, it seems that May's deal would still lack the Parliamentary numbers to pass.

What about a General Election, a change of government, and then a pivot to a Norway-style arrangement? Possibly, but whose interests is a General Election actually in? Why would Conservative MPs decide to vote to secure their own demise?

The simple free-trade agreement between the UK and the EU without all the additional trappings makes perfect sense, but there is no such proposal on the table. Without that possibility existing, so close to Brexit Day, how could it happen? Even so, would the backstop issue be resolved?

From there, many people suggest that in the absence of any agreed option, the only remaining logical outcome is a No-Deal Brexit. This I hear a lot from Brexiteers desperate for it to be so, but there is no possible majority in the House of Commons for it. There would be a majority in the Commons to prevent that from happening, and I suspect that those MPs would find that the Speaker of the Commons would look favourably on any Parliamentary motions to prevent that outcome.

With every passing month, the number of possibilities has shrunk. After October, a second referendum became almost impossible. From December, renegotiating a simple Canada-style free trade deal ran into its own time diffiulties.

We're now rapidly approaching the point where a General Election could not be held in sufficient time for an incoming Parliament to implement the result of that election. Unless there is some movement in that direction literally whilst this book is being printed, I suspect that the time will run out on that one too. Since the Fixed-Term Parliaments Act of 2011, a General Election requires one of two things:

a) Two-thirds of MPs vote for an early General Election, or
b) A motion of no confidence is passed in the government, without a new government being formed within two weeks

There is no appetite for a), largely because it would require a large number of Conservatives to vote for it against the wishes of their own Party. It is pretty safe to assume that the motion of no confidence would be the trigger.

This requires a two-week period for attempts to form a new government, followed by 25 working days for the General Election to be held.

I'm not convinced that holding a General Election on March 28th, the day before Brexit, would be practical. The count would not finish until the 29th, so I can't envisage a circumstance in which Parliament could reasonably meet or a government be properly formed in the meantime. Generally speaking, an incoming Parliament sits for the first time a few days after the election. The date is determined by a Royal Proclamation, so it's possible that this wouldn't result in delays.

If we were to pencil in a hypothetical General Election a week earlier, on March 21st (and this doesn't really seem to leave enough time for a new government to come in and take decisions - especially given the likelihood of there being another hung Parliament with the need to form alliances and coalitions), this would mean that a motion of no confidence would have to pass by the last day of January (give or take a day or so).

Admittedly, a motion of no confidence is something which could happen relatively quickly, but no matter how quickly it passes, we'd be looking at a new government taking office during March - with legislation needed to pass before Brexit. Remember that Brexit is enshrined in law for March 29th; supposing that a government were somehow elected on a Manifesto commitment to reverse Brexit, it would not necessarily even have time to enact the necessary legislation to do so. Any attempt to use the Royal Prerogative to override legislation would - thanks in no small part to the Gina Miller court case (see Chapter 7 for why this is so important) - no doubt lead to an immediate court case and legal challenge.

At the time of writing, a pre-Brexit General Election is *just about* possible. By the time of publication, it will be almost impossible. If the wheels are not set in motion by the end of January 2019, another option will be completely removed from the table.

What about Parliament voting to ask for an extension of Article 50 before a General Election is called? This would be equally problematic. A Government in the process of facing a motion of no confidence is hardly in a position to allocate Parliamentary time for the amendment of legislation on Brexit.

I'm going to assume that by the time this book is published, we still have a functioning government and that an early General Election is ruled out. By narrowing down the options, it must by definition increase the chances of the ones which haven't been eliminated - however improbable they might seem at first.

If there is no General Election, who benefits the most? There's one obvious answer to that question: Theresa May.

By running down the clock, Parliament is left with three options (or possibly four, but I'll come back to the other one) in Theresa May's own words:

- Theresa May's deal
- No deal
- No Brexit

Without a change of government, and without Parliamentary time to devote to legislation, the notion of No Brexit seems pretty much impossible. If Theresa May can remove that option from the table, she will leave Parliament with the following choices:

- Theresa May's deal
- No deal

In such a circumstance, I believe that MPs in the House of Commons would vote for Theresa May's deal.

Theresa May's deal would, in my view, be a very bad option for the country - but I suspect that if we're honest with ourselves, deep down we know that Parliament will not, when push comes to shove, vote so as to permit a no-deal Brexit.

Therefore, in my view the most likely scenario now is that Theresa May's deal will pass, much closer to the March 29th deadline. This may require a short extension (a month or so) to the Article 50 deadline and the Brexit date.

The UK will leave the European Union in the spring of 2019, but it will be a bittersweet moment for Brexiteers. The UK will have regained its freedom from the European Union, only to find that the Withdrawal Agreement constrains the UK to an extent that most would find completely unacceptable.

Theresa May would win the battle, but she would be judged harshly by both sides in the future. She would damage her own credibility and her Party's for a long time to come, tempered only by the fact that other Parties have such problems.

There is one other possibility, one which seems almost too ridiculous to point out. What if Parliament were absolutely determined to prevent the 'May's deal versus No deal' choice? Parliament, just like everyone else, can see that May is attempting to run down the clock on Brexit. Suppose that a motion of no confidence in Theresa May's government were to succeed, with the intention of preventing May's deal? Instead of triggering a General Election, a minority government were formed as a caretaker government to kick Brexit into the long grass with a General Election to follow after the delay had been forced through (rescinding Article 50 perhaps)?

Such a decision would be profound: it would go against not just the referendum but against Manifesto commitments too. I'd like to say that it can't happen, but we should never underestimate the determination of establishment politicians to propagate the establishment. There's a clue in the phrase 'establishment politicians'.

I don't think it will happen. I don't think a no-deal Brexit will happen either. Most likely (and it seems staggeringly unlikely at the moment), Theresa May will still somehow get her deal through Parliament by leaving Parliament with no other decent options.

EPILOGUE

"Nature abhors a vacuum" - Aristotle

Politics, just like nature, abhors a vacuum. If either of these results happen, it seems inconceivable that so many millions of people could continue to be completely abandoned and unrepresented.

Something will have to change, and in time it will. Political parties are born and political parties die. Under our First Past The Post system, political parties have a shelf-life far beyond the span of parties in our European neighbours. We see new parties replace the old on a regular basis across Europe in proportional voting systems. Yet even under First Past The Post, profound changes can and do happen. In Canada, the Progressive Conservative Party went from being a majority government in 1988 to just 2 seats in 1993. By 2003, the party was dissolved, having in the meantime been replaced by a new Conservative party.

It may take time, perhaps even a decade, but a change must happen. Whether that change comes in the form of a new political party, or a radical transformation of the existing parties, remains to be seen.

To many people, the coming months may feel like the death of democracy. We must not abandon our principles. If we stop believing in the power of the people to change our nation, we will ultimately stop believing in our nation altogether. We must never give up on this United Kingdom.